CIRCLE THREE TIMES
AND LAND IN CHIHKIANG

WAR TORN
CHINA 1940s

ROBERT YOST

phyost
West Palm Beach, Florida

Copyright © 2019 Patricia Yost & Evan S. Yost

ALL RIGHTS RESERVED
Printed in the United States of America

Published posthumously

The majority of images published in this narrative are from a small collection of photographs brought home by the author when returning from military service in the U.S. Army Air Corps, 1942 to 1946. The identifying annotations were limited.

(cover) Fourteenth Air Force airfield at Chihkiang, China, 1945. Incoming aircraft tail number 9635. Author, Bob Yost, pictured in the foreground.

War is too important to be left to the Generals

Georges Clémenceau

Chapters

	Foreword	i
1	Report for Duty	1
2	Luck of the Draw	3
3	On the Way ... to Where?	11
4	Crossing the Pacific	18
5	Unlike Home	22
6	Up and Over	28
7	Peishiyi and the 397th	32
8	On the Road — again	42
9	A Remote Corner	55
10	The End in Sight	72
11	What Would Follow?	78
12	Next, to Hankow	82
13	Waiting in Shanghai	89
14	Heading Home	98
	Ending Note	101
	Addendum	103
	WAR TORN CHINA - scenes	105

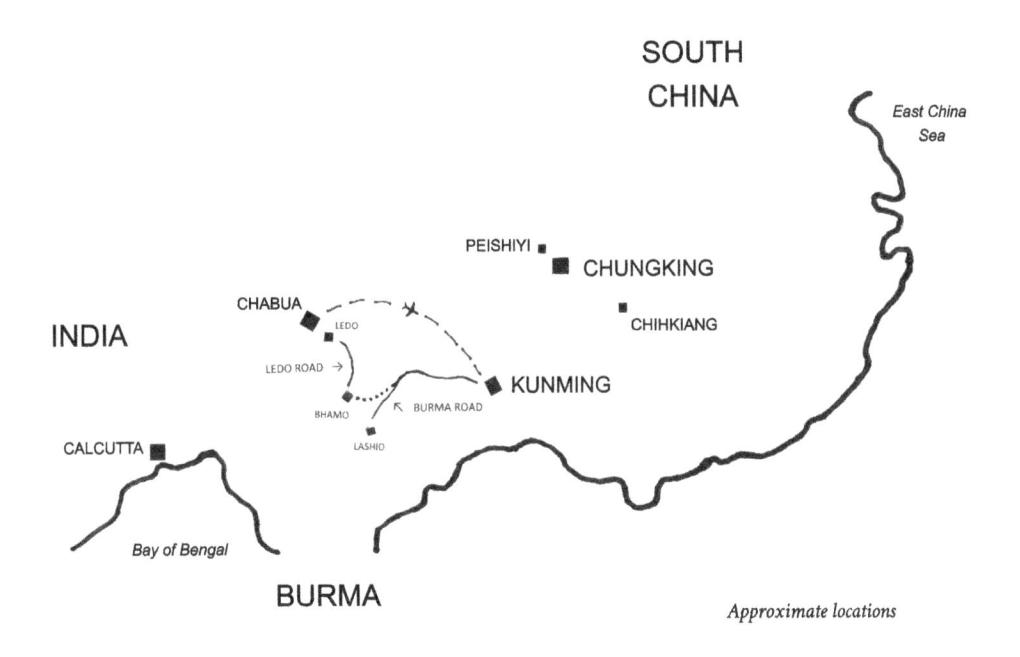

SOUTH CHINA

East China Sea

PEISHIYI ■ ■ CHUNGKING
CHABUA ■ ■ CHIHKIANG
✈
LEDO
INDIA
LEDO ROAD →
■ KUNMING
BHAMO ← BURMA ROAD
CALCUTTA ■
LASHIO

Bay of Bengal

BURMA

Approximate locations

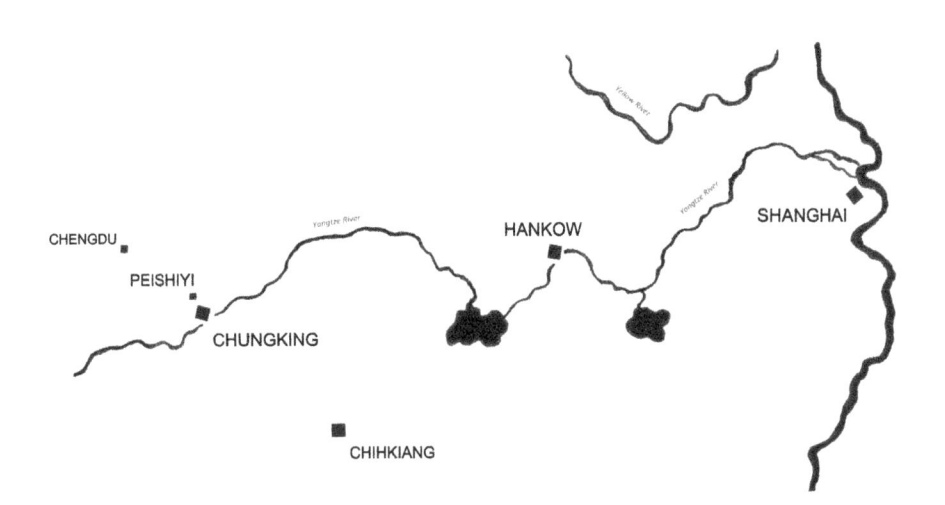

Yellow River

CHENGDU ■
Yangtze River
HANKOW ■
Yangtze River
SHANGHAI ■
PEISHIYI ■
■ CHUNGKING

■ CHIHKIANG

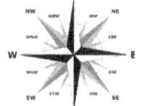

Foreword

Narratives of war are plentiful. Countless volumes have been penned, chronicling the strategies, the battles, the heroisms, the horrors.

Plentiful too are the personal memoirs — the private recollections of a formative time in someone's life; recollections buried, then pulled back into light decades later. Many of these diaries — diaries such as this one — are revealing journals of transit, the trial-by-fire trek from boyhood to manhood.

In war, the recruits who are lucky enough to see no battle and suffer no injury are nonetheless impacted by the command to serve. It is a period of life when the young and naïve grow up fast.

This particular narrative deals with a young man, barely out of his teens, who was raised in the suburbs of Long Island, New York. Up to this point, his life had been comfortable and commonplace; an average upbringing and a conventional first name: Robert. He preferred 'Bob'.

In 1942, Bob's fresh leap into married life hit full-stop with the words, "Report for a physical." He was plucked from home and fired off on a journey that he, and thousands like him, faced with mixed emotions and sobering prospects. Military service was the order of the day in the 1940s.

America was ramping up for a war — and these raw recruits were being tagged, pigeonholed, and placed on standby for the jobs ahead. Like a chip on a checker board, Bob found himself corralled with herds of other young men being shuffled from one square to the next, rarely knowing the next move. Did the officers in charge know either?

Trains transported the troops to military camps for training. Later the men were back on the trains, moving in widening circles, eventually winding up in staging areas for the final launch abroad. Akin to the family pet, they were circling around three times before settling down. Thousands were shipped to Europe, others were pointed west to Asia. Suddenly it was a big world out there, foreign and somber.

- 1 - *Report for Duty*

Denial was no longer an option. By 1941, it was becoming clear that sooner or later we Americans would have to turn our attention to the ugly realities taking place in the world. Even though our jobs, our families, and our personal lives seemed all-important at the time, the daily headlines in the newspapers told us otherwise. The situation was heavily fraught; a worldwide firestorm had caught hold and was spreading.

Day by day, we saw freedom being extinguished in Europe. Only the neutral Swiss and Swedes remained untouched. The continent was engulfed by the onslaughts of Hitler's Blitzkrieg — lands occupied, liberties abolished. Russia was next. Britain was bleeding badly, but somehow carrying on. In Asia, Japanese armies were sweeping ruthlessly through huge swaths of China and the smaller countries nearby.

In spite of the graphic stories we read in magazines and newspapers, and heard on our radios, America's focus remained determinedly inward, securely cradled — or so it seemed — by the immense Atlantic to our east and the Pacific to our west. But all of that changed in an instant in early December 1941, when Japanese aircraft struck Pearl Harbor. Four days later, Germany and Italy, too, declared war on the United States. The issue was joined. America was at war. I was twenty years old.

In June 1942, I married my high school sweetheart and moved into a newly built bungalow on Long Island, New York. Three months later, I received a card from Selective Service. "Greetings" it said, "report for a physical."

I passed the exam and swore an oath of loyalty to the United States. It was an emotional moment — unexpected, and difficult to explain. Was it a feeling of love of country, of patriotism and pride? Perhaps it was the unanticipated bond felt with other men taking the same oath, strangers soon to become fellow soldiers. This bonding of men, these deep feelings of comradeship, were ever a wonder to me during my years in service.

There also were feelings of uncertainty — forebodings of things to come. This was a serious enterprise. One could get seriously hurt, or become seriously dead. Defeating three powerful dictatorships after they had already spread-eagled their opponents in Europe and Asia was a monumental job. It also meant that hundreds of thousands of men, perhaps more, would certainly die; many more would suffer horrific wounds. Admittedly, fear had its cold hand on my shoulder, too, when I pledged my allegiance to country.

After receiving assurances from Mr. Goldman, my boss at the *New York Sun* newspaper, that I would be welcomed back to my job in the advertising department when the war was over, I said a quiet farewell to my friends. The last hours were spent with my wife, at home, as we looked around the house we had so recently settled into. My father and my reliable Uncle George then saw me off on a train headed for Camp Upton, a World War I induction center that was still operating on eastern Long Island.

- 2 - Luck of the Draw

In early November 1942, I was on a troop train headed — somewhere. No officer or non-com would disclose our destination. As the train kept rolling south, rumor after rumor proved to be false. When we passed Savannah, Georgia, it seemed clear we were headed for Florida. We were told our final stop would be Miami.

The scenes greeting us as we were transported in Army trucks from the Miami train station to the oceanfront on Miami Beach were surreal. This was a world of swaying coconut palms, blue-green water, broad beaches, women in bathing suits and shorts, formations of soldiers marching on city streets and training on lush golf course fairways. Above all, the weather was balmy, the breezes warm and inviting. These *had* to be sets from some low-budget Hollywood film.

I had been drafted into the Army and wound up in the Army Air Force. Miami Beach was an Air Force Basic Training Center set up to handle about 96,000 men at a time; the eventual goal was far greater. And for some serendipitous reason, fate decreed that I should be one of them. It was a gift straight from heaven.

Like most of my companions, I knew nothing about airplanes — I had never been in one. As a boy, I sculpted model airplanes from balsa wood, and read *Flying Aces* magazine — stories about exploits of World War I aviators, with Baron von Richthofen chief among them. That was about it.

The Air Corps was then a branch of the Army. They needed men to perform every kind of job — aircraft mechanic and pilot, radio operator and aerial gunner, officer candidate and legal affairs officer; navigator, clerk-typist, cook and baker, and men to pack parachutes. Nearly all of the recruits had to be trained for one or another of these specialties. One part of the Air Corps basic training program was testing for aptitudes.

For some illogical reason, I did very well on the test for radio operator. Since the whole idea was to select men qualified for the various Air Corps training schools, I assumed I would be assigned to radio school. Instead, because I had previously been classified for Limited Service due to a cracked vertebrae suffered in football four or five years earlier, I was offered the option of remaining at the Miami Beach training center. I quickly accepted — 'Permanent Party' it was called. It was going to be a long war. Spending some of the time in this military oasis could hardly be considered hazardous duty.

When the Air Force (still called Air Corps by the troops) surveyed the country to find a place that could be converted quickly to a training base for up to a million men, the resort hotels of Miami Beach, sited in a compact, insular location, seemed a perfect solution. In February 1942, the Air Force announced it would take over most of Miami Beach's 330 hotels — more than eighty percent of them, in fact.

By April, 70,000 rooms, large and small, were available for military use. Tourists were removed, often within twenty-four hours; Army cots and standard issue Army furniture replaced most of the hotel furniture. Golf courses became drill fields; the long sandy beaches were ideal for exercise. Mess halls were set up in neighborhood cafeterias and in hotel dining rooms. A number of temporary ones, including mine, were built on empty, barren lots.

The entire mobilization happened fast. This active training center for thousands of conscripts suddenly appeared out of nowhere. Interestingly, while all of this was going on, large portions of Miami Beach, away from the ocean and its waterfront hotels, remained home to high-rolling tourists and permanent residents. The impact on the city of Miami was negligible.

Immediately after arriving, I was assigned a room and three roommates in one of the small Air Force barracks hotels on South Beach. In the initial months of basic training, my barracks changed several times; it was easy enough to throw clothes into a duffel bag and move on. When I was made Permanent Party, I remained on South Beach, assigned to a Headquarters Company garrisoned at a hotel near fashionable Lincoln Road. Our army of occupation did little to disrupt the reign of Saks Fifth Avenue, Bonwit Teller, and other high fashion emporiums.

Symbolic of the wartime changes was the slap-dash mess hall erected on a lot at the end of Lincoln Road, near the ocean. That little corner of Miami Beach would be the center of my life for more than a year. My army residence was the Georgian Hotel; my headquarters workplace was in the National Hotel, on the corner of Lincoln Road and a very ordinary Collins Avenue. The temporary mess hall served personnel of both places. Few could have foreseen the worldwide reputation — glamour, decadence; take your pick — that this down at the heels Art Deco area of South Beach would achieve decades later.

In my group of trainees, there were men who should never have been there, many of them more than forty-five years old, a few over fifty. Nevertheless, they were drafted by some draft board that had to reach its quota. Some trainees marched or drilled with obvious infirmities — a British chap from World War I, nearing fifty, with one shoulder shot away; another man had a glass eye; others had shortened legs or withered limbs. Later, overseas, I would see men with similar problems — or worse.

On an inspection visit to Miami Beach, President Roosevelt noticed these compromised G.I.s and ordered stricter adherence to regulations having to do with age and physical condition. A blanket review led to a number of men with serious disabilities being discharged, but — as with the pendulum swinging too far opposite — many more were discharged for the slightest deviation from physical perfection. Men with flat feet were released, as were others with less than perfect vision, easily correctable with glasses. Roosevelt's review undoubtedly saved the lives of unfit men who should never have served. But, as is ever thus, the rigid interpretation of an unquestioning bureaucracy can determine who lives and who dies. Kismet often decides which role each of us plays in the Human Comedy.

Basic training was sometimes boring, seldom surprising, always tiring. We learned how to march, maneuver and turn on command, how to climb ropes and scale walls. Medics stood by in the relentless heat to treat the men who passed out. Personally, I found the marching and singing (getting better daily) was a positive part of training. It stirred the sense of connection that is essential for most men. Some of the songs were pop tunes of the day — who can remember them all. Others were more robust, ribald classics suitable only for marching men.

Mastering the carbine and the rifle, receiving medals for marksmanship in both, gave my sense of male pride another boost. Less so the kitchen duty, which brutally pierced the ego. Scouring greasy pots, and emptying and cleaning stinking garbage cans, tended to keep things in balance. The good times were usually offset by the bad, but the best times were actually okay.

Before sunrise, we awoke to rousingly vulgar calls for reveille, roll call, and announcements for the day. Running on the beach was next. Calisthenics and exercise, gas mask drill, a bugle-led flag raising, and breakfast at the mess hall completed our start-up. The flag ceremony was the most moving; gas mask drill the most deplored. Physical activities, field drills, hours on the firing range, lectures and training films rounded out the day. Most men remembered the films with loathing — especially those graphically illustrating the dangers to be avoided in more personal matters. On the whole, basic training was not an unpleasant experience, but everyone was glad when the thirteen weeks ended.

My permanent work in Miami Beach began in a small, quirky School Assignments section. Little intelligence was required to fill requisitions from training schools and air bases for a specified number of men classified in one or another of the Air Force specialties. It was all determined by classification options listed on cards we maintained for each man; usually there were three options on each card.

The best part of this power was choosing to send some decent young fellow to an air base or Air Force school near his home — sometimes to be near his wife and children, or to be close to sick parents. Sometimes these fellows found us, told us their stories; sometimes we learned about them from others. But when some breezy, loud-mouth twit or second-rate film actor came by, expecting assignment to a base or location near the Big City merely because he was a showbiz kind of guy, we often were able to ship him to an isolated Air Force school near San Antonio, or an air base in Kansas or Oklahoma. As long as we adhered to the options on the soldier's record, we were using our assigned discretion to make fair and just decisions. Or so we chose to believe.

But most men, whatever their role in civilian life, asked for no special favors as they passed through Miami Beach. Actors Clark Gable and Robert Preston attended the Officer Candidate School along with thousands of other recruits, not seeming to expect any different treatment. I noted each of them on chow lines, quietly waiting his turn.

I witnessed two phenomena in Miami Beach: first, an invasion of thousands of young female tourists; second was the local Jewish community and its culture. The invading women came by train or bus, some by car if they could get hold of rationed gas coupons. They arrived with suitcases stuffed with dresses, bathing suits, lingerie, perfume — and an infusion of raging hormones. A few hotel rooms were still available in our part of the Beach, south of Lincoln Road, as were a few small efficiency apartments, most of them outside the military zones.

The female incursion was like a shark feed, pure and simple — well, not so pure, but it was simple. The only men remaining back home were the adolescents and indispensables, the aged and infirm. In Miami Beach, at any given time, there were nearly 100,000 of them, nearly all young and fit, a great many of them unmarried. All that mattered to the arriving horde of young, and not so young, women were the targets of opportunity — thousands of them. The young men welcomed these newcomers with open arms, open wallets, and open trousers.

The reckless abandon with which these packs of somewhat less than virtuous women swarmed the streets of South Beach, confronting thousands of disbelieving young soldiers, was a sight to behold. The scene resembled Hamburg's madcap red light district more than Miami Beach. A significant number of the besieged conscripts viewed it as a large field of luscious strawberries at the peak of perfection — if not picked, the fruit would simply wither and die. The irresistible force of nature had its way; it usually does. As a newly-married man, I could only murmur: *Go get 'em, tiger.*

The South Beach where I trained, worked, and lived was not part of the more affluent Miami Beach. Despite the military presence, it remained home to a permanent population of elderly, low-income retirees — thousands of elderly Jewish men and women, mostly from New York, living in the few unglamorous hotels and small, second-class apartment buildings not taken over by the Air Force. Many of these Jews were former garment workers, first generation shopkeepers, and refugees from Europe. Thousands of them lived scattered throughout the military areas.

A vast number of Jewish restaurants, Kosher delicatessens, food and fish markets, were there to cater to them. Old men and women, mostly women, sat together in hotel lobbies or on street-level porches, playing cards or mah jong — or just kibitzing and nibbling on food purchased at the local delis. Kosher signs were seen along the length of Washington Avenue, as were men wearing skullcaps. The dominant speech of the area was Yiddish.

Most of Miami Beach was financially and ethnically segregated. Gentiles, many of them prosperous, gathered in communities well north of Lincoln Road. Some of the small hotels posted signs *Gentiles Only* and *Restricted Clientèle*. In Jewish sections, especially on South Beach, ethnic boundaries were established by signs reading *Kosher* and *Dietary Laws Observed*. Somehow this cultural and economic segregation influenced us little; it was something we noticed, then quickly forgot.

More noticeable, perhaps, was the fact that white Christians and Jews, alike, adhered to practices that kept most people of color out of Miami Beach. They were required to have identification cards issued by the Miami Beach police, complete with pictures and fingerprints. They could not rent or buy property. They had to leave the Beach before dark, returning to homes in Miami and Coconut Grove. No later political conversion can erase the near unanimity of white prejudice at that time — whether Jewish or Gentile.

Army Air Force truck convoy passing through Miami Beach, 1943 (1)

- 3 - On the Way ... to Where?

Orders came through in the spring of 1944 directing the Air Force to begin dismantling its training facilities. Left unanswered were questions of when the permanently assigned soldiers would depart and where they would be sent.

For those remaining in Miami Beach, work schedules were more relaxed, visits to the beach more frequent. The Cooks and Bakers School, and mess hall personnel in general, now had ample time to prepare elaborate meals and an astounding assortment of desserts, cakes and pies. Their work celebrated their art — it dazzled the eye and satiated the palate of even the most demanding military gourmet. Daily we were given farewells of opulence and grandeur, but it all ended quickly.

Orders were cut sending some of us to the air base at Kelly Field, near San Antonio, Texas. The pleasant months of ocean and beaches, night-blooming jasmine, gardenias and bougainvillea, were over. It had been like a glorious ride in a comfortable limousine. From now on, we would be demoted to army trucks on dusty back roads. Up to this point, I had been unbelievably lucky. Now it was time to join the real Army Air Force; and, not surprisingly, I looked forward to it. There were real wars going on out there. It was more than time to go.

After a month or two at Kelly Field, I was sent to a succession of airfields. The first was Smoky Hill Army Air Field in Salina, Kansas; then Tinker Field, outside of Oklahoma City; and later, two bases again in Kansas, at Hays, and Pratt. I had become a rootless replacement — a 'casual' as we singles were called — classified as a Sergeant clerk-typist, now anxious to fill any empty slot in a unit being prepared for shipment to the Asia-Pacific Theater. Casuals were last-in and first-out if more experienced men could be found.

On the cold spring day when our group arrived at Smoky Hill from Kelly Field, we were stunned to see row after row of astonishingly large aircraft. They were new B-29 bombers from Boeing — Superfortresses, they were called — larger by far than the workhorse B-17s that had pulverized much of German-occupied Europe. These sleek, silver birds were designed to fly long distances into the heartland of Japan, to destroy that nation's cities and military installations.

The B-29 was the most powerful, the most advanced airplane the United States had yet produced. Its existence was generally unknown outside of the military. Plans for this new heavy bomber were kept under wraps at the Boeing plant where they were built, and at training bases in Oklahoma and Kansas, where units of an entirely new Air Force — the 20th Bomber Command — were being organized.

I was assigned to an air service squadron nearly (according to rumors) ready to deploy to an island in the Marianas recently occupied by our Marines. It would be a base for B-29s, less than one thousand miles from Japan, and four hundred miles from the mainland of China. We were advised to prepare for departure from Smoky Hill at any time. At that point, I had only a vague idea of my place in this cohesive, well-trained group of men, but I was relieved to know the bird had landed — at last I was to be part of a unit with a defined mission.

Early one morning we were roused from bed, told to get ready for movement by truck convoy to Tinker Field. The news was met with general enthusiasm as we showered and shaved. Suddenly word spread like wildfire. Americans were landing in France; soldiers had parachuted into several places on the French coast of Normandy. Radios were turned on; the first incomplete reports ricocheted through the barracks. D-Day — 6 June 1944.

The news was riveting. The reported invasion would subdue the Nazis quickly, we all believed; the war in Europe would end, and the final assault on Japan could begin. In wartime, so I discovered, all things seem possible if you believe strongly enough. On this day, we were all believers.

Not only were the soldiers exuberant. Townspeople by the hundreds — then, many hundreds — lined the roads, some cheering, some weeping, as our 'mighty convoy', overflowing with equipment and gear, sped by on its way to war. Or so they (and we) chose to believe, at least for a day. Seeing troops dressed in full gear with helmets, duffel bags and backpacks created an illusion that thrilled everyone.

We felt like brave soldiers riding our stallions to the battle at Gettysburg. I certainly shared the general excitement, even though all of us knew the Air Force was merely transferring us from one base to another — from Smoky Hill to Tinker Field. It was just a tasty coincidence that our convoy rolled out on D-Day. If it made everyone feel a bit more patriotic — well, so much the better.

It became clear that my outfit was, in fact, being prepared for shipment to the Pacific. Tinker Field was a large facility able to provide the final spit and polish to the B-29s and their support units. Hearing rumors of the raging battle going on in the Marianas at Saipan, I was caught up in the general euphoria that precedes any troop movement or action.

Just as I began accepting the idea of becoming involved with the B-29 transfer to the Pacific, I was notified that I would be cut loose — replaced by a more experienced man, one formerly with the outfit. I packed my duffel bag and awaited new orders.

Papers came through, shipping me from Oklahoma to Kansas, where I spent the next few months at two air bases named for the small towns of Hays and Pratt; population at the time, five thousand or so, each. Memories of Hays are blank — nothing recorded. But Pratt is better remembered. There, for the first time, I saw miles and miles of flat cornfields in straight rows, seemingly identical in height and color. Geometrically, it was a beautiful sight. The second memory, a pleasant one, is of friendly, gracious people missing their own sons and anxious to extend warm hospitality to those of others.

Twice, after Sunday church, a friend and I were invited to dinner with families straight out of a novel or play about the Great American Heartland. These were not the emotionally gnarled, disfigured characters of a Eugene O'Neil play. Rather, they resembled less animated characters imagined by a playwright who finds goodness in his subjects. These Kansans were decent people, kindly and warm; difficult for anyone to forget.

A short time later I received papers ordering me to the Army Air Force Overseas Replacement Depot at Greensboro, North Carolina. This was the last stop for soldiers needed as replacements for overseas units; this was a place to do little more than go to reveille, salute the flag, pick up butts, and go to mess hall three times a day. It was where you simply awaited overseas assignment.

The regular system of filling requests for replacements was torn apart by the Battle of the Bulge. Beginning December 16, in heavy snow, freezing cold and fog, the German Army counter-attacked U.S. forces in Belgium through the thinly held American front in the Ardennes Forest.

The 101st Airborne Division, recalled from a rest center one hundred miles behind the lines, was surrounded at Bastogne. The Germans, believing the Airborne's situation hopeless, demanded the commander of the unit surrender immediately — to which General Anthony Clement McAuliffe issued his defiant response "Nuts." The siege of Bastogne was broken when the skies cleared and American planes re-entered the fight, dropping critically needed supplies to the beleaguered troops on the ground. The battles raged on.

The Bulge was on the verge of becoming a catastrophic defeat. Not only were thousands of American soldiers killed during that horrific battle, many others, including the wounded, froze to death. Quickly, the men on-hold at Greensboro, all trained as some type of specialist — including student pilot — were re-classified as infantrymen, given crash training, handed rifles, and air-lifted to Europe.

These poorly trained soldiers were thrown into battle and, as many writers suggest, helped to stop the German advance. What might be considered with more certainty is that too many of them died untrained for the fighting that ended their lives.

This kind of chaos has been known to all wars. Being handed a rifle and thrown into the breach, against tanks, with other untrained men, is no way for a man to die. Aware that any day I could be 'handed a rifle' and flown to Europe, I volunteered for shipment to Asia or the Pacific — to one of the B-29 bases, if possible. Within a day or two, my name was posted. Destination: the Asia-Pacific Theater of Operations. That was all I knew.

Our troop train was scheduled to depart the Replacement Depot the morning after Christmas, so a small Christmas Day party was in order, arranged by my wife (who had traveled by train from Long Island) and four Army buddies known to me for barely two or three weeks; friendships in the service were often of short duration.

On 26 December 1944, a military band — always a band — cheered our departure from Greensboro. It took five days for our train to cross the United States. Military priority on all rail transportation at the time benefited the ordinary soldier — pullman berths were available for the entire trip. Once past Atlanta, New Orleans and Houston, it was on to Dallas, El Paso and Phoenix, with a final stop at Camp Anza, about seventy-five miles from Los Angeles. After ten days of boat drills, shots, lectures and more unsavory training films warning of certain dangers to be avoided, we were ready to go. We boarded a train for Long Beach, the port of embarkation where our transport ship awaited.

General Anthony Clement McAuliffe (1)

December 22, 1944, the following note was delivered to General Anthony McAuliffe, acting commander of the 101st Airborne Division troops defending Bastogne, Belgium:

"The fortune of war is changing. This time the U.S.A. forces in and near Bastogne have been encircled by strong German armored units. More German armored units have crossed the river Ourthe near Ortheuville, have taken Marche and reached St. Hubert by passing through Hompre-Sibret-Tillet. Libramont is in German hands.

"There is only one possibility to save the encircled U.S.A troops from total annihilation: that is the honorable surrender of the encircled town. In order to think it over, a term of two hours will be granted beginning with the presentation of this note.

"If this proposal should be rejected, one German Artillery Corps and six heavy A. A. Battalions are ready to annihilate the U.S.A. troops in and near Bastogne. The order for firing will be given immediately after this two hours' term.

"All the serious civilian losses caused by this artillery fire would not correspond with the well known American humanity."

The German Commander

That same day, General Anthony McAuliffe sent his official response:

December 22, 1944
To the German Commander,
"N U T S !"
The American Commander

"The Story of the NUTS! Reply." By Kenneth J. McAuliffe, Jr.
December 12, 2012
https://www.army.mil/article/92856

- 4 - *Crossing the Pacific*

It was dusk when the crowded military train came to a halt, then disgorged several thousand soldiers on a pier in Long Beach, California. Looming in the faded light was the grey hulk of a 17,250-ton Army troop transport — the *USS General J. H. McRae*. The date was 11 January 1945.

I was one of sixteen million men in the country's military forces, a less than insignificant player in a worldwide drama affecting nearly every person on earth. But that evening on the pier — backed by yet another booming military band, and dressed in my crisp Army Air Force uniform with back pack, steel helmet, and meticulously-packed canvas duffel bag in hand — I was bursting with pride, a singular pride, as we filed up the gangplank of the *General McRae*. Smiling grey ladies of the Red Cross circulated among us, handing out sandwiches, doughnuts, and coffee. I was on my way to play whatever small part in the war I was destined to play. After more than a year in uniform, it was a relief that at last I would be doing my share.

It was obvious we were headed for the Asia-Pacific Theater. As we settled down that first night in our narrow canvas bunks, stacked four high, less than eighteen inches apart — mine being a bottom bunk next to the outside bulkhead — each man was alone with his thoughts. I quietly read the book I'd brought along, *Captain of Castile*. Sailing across the massive Pacific, to somewhere unknown, I was shipping out with other replacements — all singles, none of us part of any established unit with its reassuring friendships, group cohesions, and assigned duties. It was a lonely night. The pride and thrill of earlier hours slipped away; there was just my narrow bunk, my duffel bag, my book, and a Military Occupational Specialty (MOS) number that would determine my future assignments — and the hope that things would look better in the morning. And they did.

Perhaps a novelist could add elements of suspense to our uneventful Pacific crossing but, truth be known, the trip was more boring than dangerous. There were the usual rumors: a nearby liberty ship had been sunk; a change in course signaled lurking torpedo boats; firing of the ship's guns meant enemy subs ahead. Nothing serious really ever happened. So it was with most rumors. But the boredom was distressingly real.

Two other troop transports sailed with us from Long Beach, but no naval escorts. The *General McRae* was, nonetheless, armed with about twenty various sized gun mounts. We were told our usual running speed of about 16.5 knots was faster than any submerged submarine. That being said, if our speed slackened or if an enemy surfaced or lay in wait directly ahead, there could be some problems.

Our course took us three hundred miles south of Hawaii, then southwest to the Gilbert and Ellice Islands where we passed within sight of the alluringly-named island of Funafuti; past New Caledonia, arriving in Melbourne on our twenty-first day at sea. Only the ship's sailors were given shore leave during our three days in that peaceful city. Like sailors everywhere, they returned to ship filled with beer and tall tales of the generosity of local damsels. Given that it was wartime, with the fittest Aussie men in service elsewhere, our sailors' overblown boasts and colorful imaginations may have been close to the mark. Major Pappy Boyington, the Marine Corps ace of flying aces, briefly recounted in his book, *Baa Baa Black Sheep*, tales even more wondrous than those told by these sailors.

One way I avoided boredom was by volunteering as a lookout on the bridge — usually six hours a day. Soldiers given this duty were to look for mines, submarines, or planes that might have evaded radar. Access to the bridge, to the officers and sailors on duty there, was a pleasant change from sitting for hours on an unforgiving steel deck or lying in a tightly confined bunk. After a number of shifts on the bridge, I was enlisted in an anti-aircraft gun crew. In spite of suspicious sightings, occasional suspense, and inciting short bursts from the guns during practice drills, everything remained quiet and true to routine.

By now, word had spread that our final destination was India. After leaving Perth, we were joined by two Australian destroyers for the last leg of our journey to the sub-continent. The Indian Ocean sea lanes were near to Japanese bases in the Dutch East Indies and Burma, so our escorts treated with care anything suspicious, any floating debris, anything capable of hiding periscopes. A large abandoned raft was quickly dispatched by depth charges and gunfire. The *McRae* joined the hunt, directing its five-inch guns at the dubious thing. It hardly mattered whether or not this gunfire was only a precaution — it added some drama to an otherwise monotonous trip.

The real drama began to unfold as we approached the mouth of India's vast Hooghly River. We were sailing through a large convoy of ships flying flags from several nations, signifying the enormity of the Allied war effort in Asia, a war zone we were about to enter. I happened to be stationed on the bridge at the time, looking through powerful binoculars. I focused the glasses on an approaching boat rowed by a crew of Indian sailors. What a sight it was. Once in range, I could better see a long, open galley perhaps thirty or thirty-five feet long, free of any superstructure. It was being stroked, in perfect rhythm, by twenty-four or twenty-six regimented Indian sailors seated two by two, their long thin-bladed oars dipping into the water at precisely the same moment. They were dressed immaculately in white long-flowing robes emblazoned with a bright red sash around the waist. Each man wore on his head a red turban. A civilian river pilot and several British naval officers dressed in tropical whites came aboard the *McRae* to take the helm and navigate our ship upriver.

USS General J. H. McRae (AP-149) *was a General G. O. Squier-class ship built for the U.S. Navy in World War II, sailing from West Coast ports carrying troops to Honolulu and other Pacific Theater destinations. On 11 January 1945, she sailed from Long Beach, CA, bound for India. Troop capacity was more than 3,000. (below)* USS General G. O. Squier (AP-130), *the lead ship of her class.*

(1)

- 5 - Unlike Home

As the *McRae* steamed slowly up the Hooghly towards Calcutta, gateway to the China-Burma-India Theater of Operations (CBI), I had no idea which of these three countries — China, Burma, or India — harbored my assignment. The river began to narrow from a mile in width to a few hundred yards. Tall palm trees lined both banks, framing a series of rolling hills beyond. It was the latter part of February, the weather was warm, the air filled with the fragrance of flowers, fruit trees, and other growing things. Verdant shrubbery and colorful flowers were everywhere. Indian women clad in vivid, flowing saris walked along riverside paths, a few of them gracefully balancing earthenware jars on their heads. Everything seemed soft, seductive, sensuous. This was not some romantic film. We were in Asia.

Within a few hours, things came back into focus as we approached Calcutta. We began passing shipyards crowded with turbaned Indian workers, most of them short, thin, scruffy. This crowded stretch of river swarmed with small primitive boats filled with children anxious to dive for coins. Suffice to say, the river was quickly swamped with American coins and diving children. In this filthy, if sacred, river, thousands of Indians bathed and prayed, filled jars with water for uses at home one could only imagine. Images of the proud, red-sashed sailors who greeted us earlier gave way to a pervasive poverty everywhere — especially in Calcutta.

Continuing on, passing the city, the crowded river scenes became punctuated with a more pastoral British India defined by stately mansions, each landscaped with trimmed shrubbery and lush tropical trees lining expansive green lawns. Women smiled and waved from shaded balconies. Heady sights like these aroused the lusty spirits of thousands of healthy men who had just spent forty-two days at sea. But we could only wave back.

After debarking about sixty miles upstream, we traveled by river ferry and army trucks through the northern outskirts of Calcutta, to the sizable Camp Kanchrapara, a replacement depot and staging area. At that point most of us learned we would remain in the CBI Theater; we were to continue on into China. During three weeks of baseball, boredom, and betel nuts that stained the teeth red, we mingled with swarms of rural Indians and learned a little about their culture.

Many things in this strange, exotic land were puzzling or contradictory to young, naïve American soldiers. Should we be concerned that food would be contaminated by cooks who cleansed themselves only with handfuls of leaves and jugs of water after squatting in the fields? Our concern was dismissed by the Hindus in our group who assured us their religion dictated the use of one hand for personal care, the other hand for food handling. What then did we think when we saw a worker in our mess hall mixing meatloaf with both hands?

The local people were very gentle, very friendly. They responded warmly to overtures from Americans, and seemed pleased to converse with us. Many — probably most — of the men spoke a well-versed, heavily-accented English. The Hindu women remained apart from these conversations, but listened shyly, silently.

Near the end of our stay in the camp, I wound up in the hospital for a few days with an infected leg. When I learned that a group of Air Force personnel would be departing camp the following day for a trip farther north to the terminus for flights into China, I asked my doctor if I could leave with my friends. There were still signs of infection, so he said "no." The following morning a different doctor looked at my leg and released me. Showing him the other leg probably had something to do with it.

The group I was joining was scheduled to leave Camp Kanchrapara and travel four hundred miles on the Bengal-Assam Railway. Destination was Chabua, in the small northeast corner of India where transport planes embarked on their risky flights into China via the Hump, that narrow air corridor over the Himalayas dubbed the *Aluminum Trail*. Wreckage of planes littered the landscape.

It was in early March that we boarded the train and began traveling north through lush Bengali countryside, through a crowded land of abundant crops and villages overflowing with too many people and too many animals. The following day we entered the broad valley of the Brahmaputra River, one of the world's great waterways. Some 1,800 miles long, the Brahmaputra rises in Tibet, flows through the Himalayas before its cold, clear waters enter the small corner of India that was our final stop before flying into China.

After a train ride lasting two days and nights, the journey ended and we boarded a dilapidated flat-bed ferry to cross the great river. In our company there were several hundred British Gurkhas, the famed fighting men of mountainous Nepal. Descended from a war-like people, these men were considered by many to be the best fighters in the world; they had been part of the British army for years.

I was awed by these intelligent, compact yet profoundly sturdy men with their famed curved knives that had scared the hell out of opponents for centuries. The Gurkhas were headed for a vicious campaign being fought nearby in northern Burma, where Chinese, British, and American soldiers had turned the tide under the decisive command of General Joseph "Vinegar Joe" Stilwell. They had freed much of Burma from the Japanese a few months earlier.

Across the river we boarded a smaller-gauge train for another day's travel through the broad river plain of Assam, heading finally to the airfields of Chabua. We knew we were getting closer to the battle zone across the Naga Hills in northern Burma; bombed-out trains were scattered along our cratered route, pushed aside as the tracks were repaired.

Whenever our train stopped — and it was often — Naga tribesmen and women sifted out of the lush forests, their opened hands filled with colored stones of every shade. Assuming them to be worthless, not wanting to be gullible, I bought none and have since regretted that skepticism. Were they really uncut gemstones of some value? Years later, I came across maps indicating various types of precious and semi-precious stones were, in fact, mined in that remote area.

Myriad images of India, too many to recount in full, were seen on my trip through Bengal and Assam ... large fields of grain plowed by men and their cattle; small vegetable gardens tended by women and children using primitive ways from the earliest days of agriculture in Mesopotamia, the Fertile Crescent, the Indus Valley. Prevalent were elephants, lumbering along dusty dirt roads, cooling off in rivers and streams; horned cattle, believed to be sacred; villages, where incense rose from burning dung that fueled cooking fires everywhere and left its earthy fragrance in the food; women dressed in soft, diaphanous cotton or linen; men clothed in sturdier fabrics, more suitable for hard, dirty work.

These lasting impressions reflected much of what I observed. Passive, simple people, not believing their lives would be much improved by the hard labor their lives required, went unhurriedly about their work. Everybody and everything moved slowly — people, elephants, cattle, trains, carts — everything. It seemed as though this life had to be endured while waiting for the future incarnations their religions promised — both Hindu and Buddhist. Even on crowded city streets, sick and exhausted people would lie down on sidewalks and in alleys, making little effort to resist the onset of death. These people seemed to be living, like the ancient Egyptians, in a culture of death. Life held little promise for them. Quite simply, it was all part of a world unknown to those of us, including myself, who had previously seen little of God's treasures.

Corner of Harrison Street (Burra Bazar) and Strand Road, Calcutta, India - 1945. Clyde Waddell, photographer. (1)

Original description: "A bewildering mass of billboards at the corner of Harrison Street (Burra Bazar) and Strand Road. One of the oldest sections of Calcutta, at the foot of Howrah Bridge, it is a fine vantage point for photo-graphing the passing parade of oddly dressed natives and curious vehicles."

The South Asia Section of the Van Pelt Library, University of Pennsylvania, acquired from a bookdealer a photograph album consisting of 60 photographs of Calcutta taken most likely between 1945-1946. Mr. Waddell was a military photographer.

Source: Van Pelt Library, University of Pennsylvania

- 6 - Up and Over

Chabua Air Station was a network of airfields situated fifty or sixty miles northwest of Ledo, Assam. It was one of the bases from which Allied transport planes, mostly American, some British, flew cargo over the forbidding Himalayas and across the Naga Hills of northern Burma, to the airfield at Kunming, China. Not far away was the new Ledo Road, tortuously carved out at huge cost and loss of life by U.S. and Chinese troops, to connect with the Burma Road, the vital supply route to Kunming cut when the Japanese captured Rangoon and overran Burma in '42.

After spending a few days at Chabua waiting for the weather to clear and eating the best food the Army Air Force could provide, my comrades and I were given survival instructions and parachutes in case our C-46 transport plane crashed in the snow-covered mountains, not an uncommon event.

This was to be my first flight, ever. Boarding the plane, we all understood that if we did crash, there would be little chance of survival; rescue was virtually impossible. We sat on long rows of metal bucket seats bolted to each side of the plane. Oxygen masks were at the ready.

As the plane circled and gained altitude, I noted that the Chabua airfields were sited in what appeared to be an enormous regional cul-de-sac, surrounded on three sides by high mountains. To the west lay Bhutan and Nepal; to the north, beyond the Himalayas, was the great plateau of Tibet — and even farther north were the more remote provinces of China. To the east were the dense jungles and mountainous ranges of Burma, a few of them reaching heights up to 20,000 feet. We may not have flown over the highest peaks in the Himalayas, but we clearly could see them.

Arriving in Kunming, I was assigned to the Fourteenth Air Force, operational only in China. After a week or so, I was flown to another air base near the small town of Peishiyi, about twenty miles from Chungking, the remote wartime capital of Nationalist China. There I discovered I had become a distant participant in the Flying Tigers' history — the original American Volunteer Group that became legendary for its daring exploits and colorful personalities. It had been a part of the armed forces of China during the first days and months of World War II.

The American Volunteer Group (AVG) was a band of military personnel recruited early in 1941 from among aviators in the Marine Corps, the Army Air Corps (later the Air Force), and the United States Navy. President Roosevelt quietly eased the way for these men to resign their commissions in the American services, then sign one-year contracts to fly as volunteers for the embattled Chinese government. Counting the ground crews and other pilots recruited in Asia (some of them soldiers of fortune), nearly three hundred men formed the first group of volunteers. It has been written that these men — and three nurses — volunteered to serve under an 'unknown' leader and fight for an 'unknown' government.

That leader was General Claire L. Chennault, a craggy-faced, tough old bastard who, upon retiring from the Army Air Corps in 1936, had signed on as an advisor to the Chinese Nationalist government of Generalissimo Chiang K'ai-shek. In its long, brutal war with Japan, China needed to build a small but effective air force. That difficult job was given to Chennault.

Four years later he organized the AVG and gained Roosevelt's approval to buy one hundred P-40 fighter planes in a convoluted deal with Great Britain via Lend-Lease, at a cost of three million dollars. The planes were to be flown by the small band of pilots Chennault recruited. By December 1941, the AVG was ready to fly missions against the Japanese from a Chinese airfield near Kunming, and another one in Burma. The airmen branded themselves the Flying Tigers and painted the familiar sharks tooth insignia on the cowlings of their airplanes. Thirteen days after Pearl Harbor, they flew their first mission — a defensive action against Japanese bombers.

But very few of the original group still remained. Some of them had been inducted into the China Air Task Force, an American military unit, successor to the AVG. Most returned to their original services. The Flying Tigers initial complement of one hundred P-40s — reduced to less than sixty through combat losses and accidents — was expanded by the addition of new pilots fresh from flight school and by new P-40s and bombers. March 1943, the China-based Fourteenth Air Force was created, Major General Chennault, commanding. The Flying Tigers, enlarged and reinforced, survived the organizational confusions of these transitions, as did their traditions and spirit, their insignia — and their swaggering indifference to discipline.

U.S.-built Army trucks seen winding along the side of the mountain over the Ledo supply road from India into Burma. (1)

Chabua airfield, Assam, India, 1944 (2)

Identities unknown

-7- *Peishiyi and the 397th*

After being interviewed in Kunming, I was assigned to the 397th Air Service Squadron, a veteran outfit whose job it was to service planes stationed at its main base at Peishiyi and at several small satellite landing strips, each manned by one or two, sometimes three, men. They were part of an early warning network devised by Chennault to protect Kunming and Chungking. The lines separating opposing armies were very fluid; everybody was behind everybody else. In addition to providing early warnings of approaching Japanese planes, these outriders did whatever they could to repair damaged American and Chinese planes — change tires, patch holes, supply fuel — enabling the aircraft to return to base safely. It was dangerous work.

It wasn't long before I realized that I had become part of a very different Air Force than I had known in the States. The 397th Squadron (12th Air Service Group) had been in China for more than two years, since the earliest days of the Fourteenth Air Force; some units dated back to the preceding China Air Task Force. They shared the personality and truculence of General Chennault. They felt forgotten. Nobody worried about them being rotated home.

Before joining the 397th in Peishiyi, I had a few days to look around Kunming. I saw and smelled — alternatively sickened and dazzled by — the faded remains of a very old civilization. Kunming was a place both of wonder and of human degradation, as was probably true of most of China's bomb-damaged cities. This was an old city, the capital of Yunnan province, crowded with refugees from the fighting that had taken place throughout southern China. It had been bombed, devastated, and impoverished but never defeated by years of war.

In spite of the city's disintegration, the Chinese people — with their open, radiant smiles and bad teeth — captured my mind, and later my heart. They toiled to the limits, trying to overcome relentless challenges and long-term poverty. Many of them remained cheerful with few reasons to be so. They had little of India's passivity; instead they struggled to counter the dreadful fate history had imposed on them. While there was underlying poverty and despair, there remained the dignity of a great civilization.

It was sad to see countless young women, and younger girls, coping as best they could, offering their only commodity for sale on a street of shame, or in brothels, as was recalled by Theodore H. White in his 1978 autobiography, *In Search of History*. It was a scene I was to see repeated often during my time in China. A few government officials, military leaders, and other prosperous Chinese, were better able to cope with the circumstances, but the majority of people had for centuries known only poverty. Now the war with Japan had made things far worse.

I found it difficult to describe, later, the many scenes I saw in Kunming, and elsewhere in China; photographs told a better tale. I brought home a small collection of them — some taken by me, some taken by other men of the 397th. These spontaneous images recorded how close to the brink most Chinese people had descended; millions more did not survive, suffering a dreadful fate at the hands of the Japanese.

On 4 April 1945, I was flown about four hundred miles north from Kunming to Peishiyi, where most 397th personnel were stationed. The previous summer, a Japanese offensive had driven the Chinese army out of southeast China and forced the American air force to evacuate its bases at Kweilin and several other locations. Fighters and bombers returned to older bases farther west, including the one at Peishiyi. Chinese Air Force planes were stationed at Peishiyi as well; most of their aircraft were of the same type used by American pilots.

Two Air Force service squadrons operated at Peishiyi — the 397th, and one staffed entirely by Chinese-American personnel who could easily communicate with the Chinese, and were better able to service the Chinese planes. These men were talented card players, too, regularly reducing to penury many of my friends. Our Asian-American comrades never encountered problems, as did others in the squadron, conducting black market activities with the local people. The non-smokers among our group regularly sold to the Chinese houseboys the two cartons of cigarettes allotted each man in his monthly rations at the Post Exchange. Some men went far beyond selling cigarettes. Occasionally they sold jeeps and trucks filled with aviation fuel. Who were the buyers, I wondered?

Our airfield received an inadequate trickle of supplies from India via transport planes flying over the Hump. As a supply sergeant, my job was to keep records on the 397th's own equipment and to order from India whatever was needed. We were told that total supplies flown over the Himalayas rarely exceed 15,000 tons a month, but I later read (and never believed) that by the end of the war, supplies reaching China from India totaled 80,000 tons monthly. If requisitions were urgent, they were conveyed directly to the States for speedy "Red Ball"* shipment, to be sent by way of our fragile lifeline. In some mysterious way that I never understood, a few requisitions were sent to our Japanese enemies. These were usually filled, quickly. Sometimes we reciprocated. Money must have been involved. It was a very strange war.

Life in Peishiyi was typical of army life everywhere in China. I went to work each day, did my job, ate three dreadful meals a day that were laced with Atabrine to combat malaria, and (it was believed) saltpeter to restrain male lust. Atabrine turned our skins dark yellow. I have no idea what the saltpeter accomplished, if anything.

The South China weather was unbearably hot, with torrential rains and monsoons in the late spring and early summer. Daytime temperatures frequently rose to 110 degrees. Our work day began at 6:00 a.m., finished at noon. Usually it felt too hot to go to the mess hall for lunch, seldom was the meal worth the effort. But we had to eat. After lunch, we generally sacked out until late afternoon when the heat quieted down.

Like most units in the interior of China, we lived off the land, as poor as it was. We suffered through endless bowls of gritty rice and bean sprouts, those incessant bean sprouts. Usually the water buffalo meat was too tough to eat, but when chewed, then discarded, it provided a tasteless juice having some dubious value. After seeing the meat brought from farms to the mess hall after butchering — dragged through dirt and dust along raised footpaths between rice paddies by bedraggled farmers who repeatedly spat and hawked and cleared their throats and nostrils on the path ahead — it clearly lost its appeal.

Eggs were always abundant and worth eating, if not the Grade A type available at home. Sometimes we had boiled onions and string beans. There was more than enough tea and coarse brown sugar in which various kinds of debris was usually found — dirt, husks, small pebbles, sometimes the remains of manure.

The one American luxury we savored was hot coffee, available most days in spite of strict limits on the tonnage flown in from India. My weight dropped from over 200 pounds to a healthy, and hungry, 172 pounds. Soon I responded to "Slim."

As a replacement coming into a veteran outfit that had been through some rough times together during the past two years — especially when they were forced by the Japanese to evacuate Kweilin and other southeastern bases — I expected to be on my own for a while. Instead, I was given a grudging welcome; many a hand was extended to me. These hard men showed little emotion. They had bonded because of their shared experiences, because they were among roughly 12,000 American soldiers, mostly Army Air Force, scattered around in a massive sea of Chinese — and because that is the way many men act in wartime. Like Scottish clansmen, some of my comrades may not have liked one another; sometimes they argued and fought physically among themselves. But always they remained bonded. I had joined the clan. I wore their badge. I was an American. That's all that mattered.

Most days we looked like, dressed like, anything but American soldiers. Many of us dressed for maximum comfort —

G.I. shoes, fatigue pants, cotton tee shirts, sometimes undershorts only. Often faces remained unshaven for days or weeks until word was passed, "shape up." When directives were issued ordering an improvement in appearance, or if a senior officer was expected from headquarters in Chungking, we more closely conformed to regulation dress code. Generally, however, enlisted men found a way to beat the system and the heat.

It must be remembered that our unit wore its heritage on its sleeve. Not only was it the CBI patch and Flying Tigers insignia. The Tigers were General Chennault's boys. He had conceived their mission, sold the idea personally to President Roosevelt. He had hammered the unit together, free of outside discipline or influence; a breed apart. And now, as an independent-minded, cantankerous old curmudgeon thoroughly disliked by his superiors, Chennault resisted the system still. He was Commanding General of the Fourteenth Air Force. We were his men.

Inspections, when they occurred, seldom achieved the results desired. Almost always, enlisted men devised ways to confound efforts by colonels and generals to improve performance. My own military experience confirms the general opinion that sergeants ran the army. One event illustrates the point when Theater Commander General Wedemeyer was scheduled to inspect our airfield at Peishiyi. In preparation, a senior supply sergeant went through our warehouses, ordering all items be stored in accordance with regulations, that they be classified and marked properly. Anything that could not be so handled and properly classified, anything that would disrupt the neat appearance of our warehouses, should be thrown into a nearby lake. A supply master sergeant was to be obeyed. Very quickly, the 397th supply warehouses took on an orderly appearance while the level of a small lake nearby rose imperceptibly.

When General Wedemeyer inspected the area, everything appeared to be neat and in good order. The General was pleased. The sergeant was pleased. The 397th was commended. Everybody was satisfied. Any important aircraft parts that might be needed could always be ordered — Red Ball.

Lt. General Albert Wedemeyer (left) seemed satisfied that all was in good order at the Peishiyi air base.

---

* Use of the term *Red Ball* to describe express cargo service dated at least to the end of the 19th century. Around 1892, the Santa Fe railroad began using it to refer to express shipping for priority freight and perishables. Such trains and the tracks cleared for their use were marked with red balls.
https://en.wikipedia.org/wiki/Red_Ball_Express

Tricks of all kinds were common. One officer who was a pleasant, forever smiling fellow involved with the 397th's supplies and equipment, hired forty or fifty extra Chinese civilians to do carpentry work. Or so the books showed. In truth, these men were experienced woodcarvers who then produced scores of refined works of art in the Chinese style, which somehow, I suspect, made their way back to the States. Stories like this were legion.

A number of men in my outfit, removed for more than two years from the disciplines of civilized life, had gone to seed. When I joined the 397th, they were deep in the interior of China, nearly one thousand miles from the coast at Shanghai, about seven hundred miles from Hong Kong. Their only connection with the outside world consisted of the precarious lifeline over the Himalayas — C-46 cargo planes bringing the barest essentials to men living a spartan life — and the truck convoys slogging over the Ledo/Burma Road after it opened in early '45 to augment the airborne supply route from India.

After two years of virtual isolation, the strands of civil behavior that held most men together weakened and, in some cases, broke. The only liquors available, except for an infrequent bottle of whiskey bought at a high price from India-based pilots, were a coarse vodka and the local jing-bao juice, a fiery concoction that sometimes led men to engage in senseless behavior. In one case, a member of our group drank deadly aviation fuel. (He eventually recovered.) At some point, about ten of our estimated 125 men were confined to the China Theater Stockade No. 1, in Kunming, for various offenses from trivial to capital; a fact I can confirm with some certainty. Yet considering the difficult circumstances and prolonged isolation, most men of the 397th behaved in exemplary fashion. They were not always dressed according to the rules; their discipline was often fragmentary. They probably drank too much and, yes, some behaved foolishly. But the vast majority were good men, good soldiers and, many of them, good friends.

Many soldiers assigned to Peishiyi, including the author (left), dressed for maximum comfort in South China's relentless heat and humidity.

*HQ, 397th Air Service Squadron
12th Air Service Group
Peishiyi air base, China*

Identities unknown

- 8 - On the Road — again

The men in my squadron, and others like them, shared an isolated continent with more than one million Japanese soldiers and more than half a billion Chinese men, women, and children suffering from every kind of disease, famine, poverty and human degradation. The ones who survived were subjected to massacre by invading Japanese and abuse from their own countrymen — warlords, government officials, and bandits. Some tax collectors extracted more from the farmers than the value of the crops.

In 1937, the Japanese-inflicted bloodbath at Nanking scarred the country and its people for years and forced the removal of Chiang K'ai-shek's government from Nanking to Chungking, deep in the country's interior. This was the China in which the 397th operated.

By the time I joined the unit in early 1945, the military balance had shifted and, for a while, it seemed the Japanese threat had lessened. But in the spring of 1945 the Japanese renewed their offensive in central China, advancing to the west in the fertile region north of the Yangtze River.

Early in the summer, we were ordered to prepare for movement to an airfield farther south; our large equipment was sent onward by air. With all men and some remaining gear loaded on army trucks, we left Peishiyi and began a hard and tedious seven-day journey through southern China's mountains, basins and rice paddies, and along a watershed valley of the mighty Yangtze.

Our convoy inched along winding dirt roads that crawled over and through an endlessly changing mountainous terrain, with unrelenting hairpin turns hacked out by bulldozers, sometimes ten horseshoes in one steep, perpendicular mile. The roads laced precariously back and forth, up and down the sides of vertical mountains and hills; sadly, a few trucks and men were lost to accident. Our destination was Chihkiang, about two hundred eighty miles south and east of Chungking, in the western reaches of China's southern Hunan province.

At the time, few people outside of China had heard of Chihkiang; I certainly had not. Yet in the early summer of 1945 it was the Fourteenth Air Force's largest forward base south of the Yangtze River, one of several playing a major role in checking the latest advance of Japanese land forces in central China.

Though I was not sure where, exactly, Chihkiang was, I thought it might be near Chengdu, with its five airfields, long runways, and remaining squadrons of B-29s. These aircraft had been grouped together in the newly created 20th Bomber Command headed by General Curtis LeMay. Their initial mission, dubbed Project Matterhorn, was to bomb the home island of Japan into ruins.

When the huge Superfortresses suffered greater losses than expected on the return runs over hostile Chinese territory, the bombing raids were sharply reduced. In the fall of 1944, soon after the Marines captured Saipan, in the Marianas, the B-29s were transferred to quickly-built island bases and, by November, began major raids on Japan. My outfit from Smoky Hill and Tinker Field had, in fact, gone to Saipan as rumored, and suffered casualties.

My fix on Chihkiang's location was entirely wrong. Leaving Peishiyi, our truck convoy followed the road south, not north, first traveling the short distance to Chungking. This wartime capitol was a pitiful sight, heavily damaged by Japanese bombs and now harboring a population swollen by refugees to well over one million people. Yet the multitude of men and women, wearing faded, but generally clean clothing, moved about from place to place, seemingly with purpose, performing simple tasks common to the Chinese people. Barbers tended to customers seated outdoors on city streets; charcoal-fired braziers were manned by women cooking and selling rice and chicken parts; ironmonger hammered out tools and utensils; dry foods and cotton fabrics were peddled in small shops and stalls, of which there were many.

The streets were one continuous, crowded bazaar. There were beggars and prostitutes, people with festering sores and running noses. And something new to me — large dead rats tied by their tails to bamboo staves and sold as food for the poor in side streets and alleys. I saw this scene repeated in other small cities and towns. To someone passing through, the people of Chungking seemed to be suffering as badly as those in Kunming and in the countryside. But amid the poverty there were moderately affluent people, too — government and party officials, men working in banks, tax collectors, small businessmen, and military officers, some living on the profits of war.

At Chungking, our convoy crossed the great river of southern China — the Yangtze. For a day or two we moved slowly along a road bordering the river, gaping at the spectacular gorges lining both sides of it. Coursing almost four thousand miles from its source high on the plateau of Tibet, down to the East China Sea at Shanghai, the Yangtze revealed to us a magnificent force of nature.

There was vigorous life on the river — families living on raft-like flat bottom boats that drifted easily with the tide, steered manually by oars and poles. Floating against the river's strong flow, the boats were pulled by men hauling on ropes. Like beasts of burden, they struggled along shoreline footpaths, straining every muscle in their nearly cadaverous bodies; leaning forward, sweating profusely in the heat — stripped to shorts and sandals — using every bit of strength they had to move their boats forward, yard by tortuous yard. This was the way many families lived, the way goods and animals were transported on China's longest river. It seemed a metaphor for all of the poor of China.

It took days for our caravan to wind through southern China. The Japanese army had not reached this part of the country, but their planes had bombed its cities and river traffic, and destroyed much of its industry. Like so much of China at the time, this agricultural heartland was isolated from the outside world, no longer refreshed by the energies and goods that normally flowed from eastern cities and the seas beyond. The people in this region were cut off from nearly everything that could improve their lives or reduce their burdens. I realized that they and their revered ancestors had probably lived similar lives for hundreds or thousands of years; lives now worsened by war, but in many ways the same as ever.

Yet these gentle, industrious and orderly people had the ability to smile easily, to be friendly. They were not formed by opposing Nationalist or Communist philosophies but were descended from an earlier, greater civilization — the dynasties of Imperial China. Although the physical world they lived in had deteriorated since the centuries of old Cathay, these people, their culture and refined philosophies, were descended from a society far more advanced than that of Europe during its Dark Ages.

Artisans, builders, and craftsmen from earlier days had left their marks on the part of China we were passing through. In the midst of ruin, there was still beauty — in the graceful architecture, in faded silk robes, in the prevailing gentle politeness. Even in the present circumstances, the people existed within a recognizable framework of civilized life.

As our small caravan continued south and east, we passed growing signs of cholera or plague, or typhoid fever. Some of the sick dragged themselves on hands and knees, their arms raised up to us; we saw dead and decaying bodies sprawled awkwardly in ditches. There was nothing we could do to help — there were just too many. China had hardened us to their suffering. Our trucks drove on.

Rice paddies were everywhere. They curtained the sides of hills and small mountains in ever ascending terraces crisscrossed by raised pathways separating the fields of one farmer from another. These networks were the connective tissue of the Chinese countryside, given that families in small hamlets and compounds outnumbered villagers. We watched women patiently planting seedlings in fields flooded, level by level, by the same primitive foot-pedal system used in Egypt three and four thousand years ago. Globalism is not a new concept.

Sometimes when our trucks stopped for the night at a hostel in a small town or village (*eating* and *sleeping* provided by our military), soldiers would respond to shy, giggled invitations from young ladies. We tend to think of such actions as prostitution, but to people struggling to survive — simply to eat — there seemed nothing sordid about it.

On one occasion, I sat in a living room of sorts in a small, ordinary house and shared a cup of tea with a quiet, middle-aged lady. She was acting as chaperon while a few of my buddies and their young ladies were elsewhere on the premises. In that tiny, isolated town, seldom were there opportunities offering rich rewards for so brief a time. The parents and their daughters had elaborate codes of honor that might temporarily be set aside, but doubtfully ever forgotten.

At one of our nighttime pit stops, a number of us shared an episode that most Chinese accepted as normal. Finished with dinner, we were directed to a long wooden barn filled with folding cots — fifty to seventy-five of them. Each man chose his bed for the night, spread a blanket, stripped to his shorts, and dozed off. The calm was broken by a bolting tribe of screeching rats racing along the rafters, jumping one beam to another, bounding from bed to bed, running across our bodies, undeterred by roars of profanity from startled men. Several rodents landed on me, on my shoulders and groin; one or two ran over my face. A surrender was declared, leading all of us to sleep under the stars for the rest of the night.

Locations unknown

Locations unknown

Transport throughout the CBI Theater was seldom routine

Locations unknown

The streets of Chungking and other Chinese cities were one continuous, crowded bazaar. People moved from place to place with purpose while performing everyday tasks ... barbers, dentists, food vendors, iron mongers, shoe makers, repair men.

Locations unknown

Locations unknown

Locations unknown

The Chinese people worked tirelessly, trying to overcome unimaginable, everyday challenges. Many of them remained cheerful, with seemingly little reason to be so.

Locations unknown

- 9 - A Remote Corner

Our convoy reached Chihkiang after seven tough days on the road. With all the twists and turns, we probably drove four hundred miles or more to cover a distance of maybe two hundred fifty as the crow flies. This remote base was serving as an 'aircraft carrier' stationed in the reaches of nowhere, anchored in the lee of the Xuefeng mountains to the west, and defined by wide swaths of low hills and arid flat basins.

We believed we were in Chihkiang to defend the base at Chengdu. Later, it seemed our mission became one to defend against a Japanese offensive aimed at Chihkiang itself. (*The Japanese did, in fact, launch an offensive for Chihkiang in early April 1945, to lay open approaches to the major cities of Kunming and Chungking. They were beaten back by Chinese fighters and forced to retreat two months later, in early June.*) But by the early summer of 1945, with the B-29s transferred to the Marianas in the Pacific, and the Japanese offensive a failure, we felt ourselves alone out there.

Nevertheless, we continued to maintain the airfield and service the reliable P-40s along with the newer, powerfully built P-47 Thunderbolts, P-51 Mustangs, and a number of B-24 Liberator bombers. As at Peishiyi, the Air Transport Command's planes flying over the Himalayas landed and spewed out cargoes of supplies from India. Aircraft of all kinds were using the field; after a while it became routine.

Planes came and went, mostly American, some Chinese. The supply staff, including myself, showed little interest in any of it. Occasionally P-40s or P-47s celebrated their combat victories by performing barrel-roll maneuvers before landing. That usually did get our attention.

We were isolated from anything other than the war and our Chinese surroundings. Shortwave Army broadcasts reported news of successes in Europe, General MacArthur's progress in the Philippines, the great naval victory at the Battle of Leyte Gulf, the firebombing of Tokyo — and the popular music on Armed Forces Radio, played by a fellow named Lenny Bernstein and his band. (After the war Leonard Bernstein got himself a *real* band.)

A more noteworthy local happening was the unexpected appearance on base of several Belgian Catholic nuns; they came from a convent a few miles away. The veterans of our outfit were not surprised by anything — ever. They had seen it all, including other missionaries and nuns in eastern China before the 397th was driven out of Kweilin. But a few of us considered it remarkable that any of these gentle women had remained in such a remote part of the country, an area where not many Westerners, other than missionaries, had been seen before the war

The nuns told us their charges — young Chinese novices — were skilled at crafting handsome embroidery; they would make gifts for those of us who had befriended them. Damaged silk parachutes somehow found their way out of our supply room and, in return, small scarves, skillfully embroidered with classic Chinese designs, somehow found their way back.

We tried to offer these cheerful young women anything we could beg, borrow or steal — well, maybe not the latter. These saintly nuns kept nothing for themselves. Everything went to the many Chinese children in their care, most of them orphaned. My closest friend in the 397th became the nuns' best source for American goods and gifts, a supply sergeant virtually on loan to the monastery. This man whom I shall call Sidney was a religious Jew from New York City, a kind man with a big heart. He would come into my life a bit later, unexpectedly.

Chihkiang was not all work and boredom. A couple of friends and I spent evenings developing the personal photographs we were taking, along with some film negatives exchanged with several of the old-timers in the outfit. Some of these pictures went back a few years, including those taken when the 397th was stationed at Kweilin, some of them showing Kweilin's remarkable rock formations famous among contemporary visitors and, in centuries past, Chinese artists and travelers.

It would be an understatement to say our system for developing film was less than primitive. A hand-made wooden light box was hammered together, housing an ordinary light bulb of uncertain wattage, connected to a frayed extension cord that led to a generator. One or two developing trays and a packet of photo printing paper were borrowed from the supply warehouse; a bit of developing fluid was purloined from the Air Force photo lab. Soon the images were rolling out. (Regrettably, a number of the more spectacular ones brought home to the States have disappeared over the years — along with the nuns' handsome embroideries.)

During this time, thousands of Chinese laborers were hard at work repairing and extending the length of our runway. With nothing more than primitive rakes, pickaxes and mallets, and small bamboo baskets swinging from flexible staves balanced across one shoulder, these resourceful people — men, women, some children — moved rocks and dirt from one place to another, gradually building up the landing strip's smooth surface. They sat patiently, in groups, hammering large rocks into little ones. Scores of laborers hauled massive stone rollers, four or five feet high, across the runway's surface to complete their work. It was an amazing undertaking and an astounding accomplishment.

The author, at Chihkiang Air Base, Hunan, China -1945

Aircraft tail number 478801

When built in 1942, the airfield at Chihkiang was used as part of the China Defense Campaign (1942-45). It also was HQ for the Chinese-American Composite Wing, jointly commanded by both American and Chinese air force officers, and manned by American and Chinese pilots and crew. The facility was closed in October 1945. Conversion of the airport for civilian use began in 2002, and was reopened as Huaihua Zhijiang Airport (Hunan Province) in 2004.

(author's notation) "A partial view of the tent area at Chihkiang. The shower room and water tower are in foreground. Rice paddy at left. A C-46 hit one night while we were asleep and burned on hill just above our tent." *Forty-four passengers and one crewman died in that crash, 30 October 1945.*

Water tower at Chihkiang Air Base

(author's notation) "Operations & Control Tower. 870 is our elevation. Officer at left, on motorcycle, is Capt. Stiles, Supply Officer."

The author (right) stands with a fellow G.I. outside their living quarters at Chihkiang Air Base, Hunan, China.

Chihkiang Air Base, Hunan, China - 1945

(author's notation) "With pride I show you our Corps Supply Office at Chihkiang. Those are belly tanks at left, for long-range fighter missions. Old Chinese graves at left. I work in left side of the building."

At work on the Chihkiang airfield, Hunan, China

(author's notation) "Typical group of locals working on the runway. With their baskets they move mountains and fill in swamps to build the runway. Just thousands of them."

The Boeing B-29 Superfortress was the most expensive aircraft project undertaken by the U.S. in World War II. Flown in the Pacific Theater by the 20th Bomber Command, these massive planes initially operated out of bases in India and around Chengdu, China. Logistical problems, range limitations, and substantial loss of aircraft soon made it impractical to continue operations as such. With the summer 1944 capture of the Mariana Islands by U.S. Marines – bringing Tokyo and other strategic targets within effective range of the B-29 – the bombers were transferred to five quickly-constructed bases in the Pacific to begin launching major raids on Japan in the final year of the war.

The remote airfield at Chihkiang served as an 'aircraft carrier' stationed in the western reaches of nowhere, isolated from anything other than the war and the remote China landscape. Seen in the far distance is the airfield's Operations & Control Tower.

"Tiger Fleet" seen painted on the forward section of the fuselage.

At the Fourteenth Air Force bases throughout southern China, heroic effort and ingenious skill went into keeping the group's aircraft serviced and in flying condition.

Identities unknown

Identities unknown

The author, standing with a B-25 Mitchell bomber at Chihkiang. Note (above) the 12-pointed white sun insignia of the Nationalist Chinese Air Force. (below) On the aircraft's nose, a visible tribute was made to Mabel.

Unidentified, but valiant still. Belly tank still attached.

Aircraft tail number 478280

The Chinese-American Composite Wing (CACW), a special fighter unit assigned to General Chennault's Fourteenth Air Force, was composed of Chinese and American pilots, crews, and support personnel serving under joint command. The group operated out of a number of bases in China, including Chihkiang. All U.S. pilots were rated in the Chinese Air Force and authorized to wear both U.S. and Chinese air force wings.

Unidentified

- 10 - The End in Sight

The weather was insufferably hot. The war in China was droning on. The center of action had moved to the Pacific where our marines were island-hopping their way to Japan — at Tarawa, Guam, Iwo Jima, Okinawa. To the veterans in my outfit, only one thing mattered ... going home. They were a spent force. But they knew there had to be an American invasion of Japan to compel surrender; it seemed unlikely my unit would be relieved until then. The hot summer was passing, with little change from day to day, with no inkling that our world was set to be turned upside down.

It was 9 August 1945; I was quietly writing a letter to my wife. A friend rushed in to give me news just broadcast on Army radio: a large bomb had been dropped on a Japanese city — Hiroshima was the name. The bomb supposedly had an explosive force comparable to 20,000 tons of TNT.

I recall my reaction. Who could forget such a moment? I thought that if it had actually happened, our people must have harnessed the atom. The idea seemed preposterous — but it was quickly confirmed. Then came further reports: a second bomb had been detonated over Nagasaki. The American military command ordered Japan to surrender, immediately and without conditions.

We were shocked. But there was no celebration, no serious debate, no talk of victor and vanquished. These gaunt soldiers, long removed from any civilized society, just wanted to go home. To them, nothing else mattered. Nothing. They showed no more interest than when President Roosevelt died the previous April.

Within days word was received, and confirmed: the Japanese agreed to surrender — unconditionally. All over China there was confusion about the way the surrender was to be negotiated. The Russians already were moving into Manchuria and Mongolia, overseeing local Japanese surrenders. In the north and some parts of the south, well-organized Communist cadres, both military and civilian, controlled large areas of the countryside and were rapidly extending their influence among the local masses.

Soon we caught wind of a rumor that a Japanese army delegation would fly to Chihkiang to conduct preliminaries for the surrender of all army forces in the China Theater. This was to take place with representatives of Chiang K'ai-shek's Nationalist government and the American Army. Few men in the 397th believed such a ridiculous report. Why would a momentous event like that take place at Chihkiang? There were nearly a million Japanese soldiers to be disarmed and repatriated. The surrender would take place at a larger city, we were certain; in a more populated location. No doubt about it.

On 21 August 1945, I was among the group of American and Chinese soldiers gathered near Chihkiang's tiny air control tower, all eyes scanning the afternoon sky, awaiting the arrival of a single, unarmed Japanese airplane. A small speck finally was spotted in the distance. As the twin-engine aircraft approached the airfield, its fuselage camouflaged in several shades of green, the Rising Sun insignia clearly visible.

When the harmless-looking plane landed and came to a stop, four grim-faced Japanese envoys climbed from the plane and formally saluted two American officers and one Chinese. Two of the envoys wore regular field uniforms, one wore civilian clothes and a straw hat, and one — obviously the leader of the delegation — was decked out in well-shined cavalry boots, a tropical pith helmet, and several feet of braid that flowed from his uniformed shoulders. With the haughty manner of a victor — not the look of the vanquished — they ignored the two or three American officers standing nearby armed with pistols and carbines.

The Japanese emissaries crowded into an American jeep driven by a helmeted Chinese soldier. A white flag of truce fluttered above the hood. Each man looked straight ahead, each face frozen stock-still.

Major General Takeo Imai, Vice-Chief of the General Staff of the China Expeditionary Army (Imperial Japanese Army), was received by General Hsiao Yi-shu, Chief of Staff of the Chinese Army Headquarters, and more than one hundred Chinese and Allied officers. The Japanese general was handed a memorandum to initial and transmit to General Yasuji Okamura, commander of Japanese military operations in China. The document stated the measures to be taken for the unconditional surrender of all Japanese forces in China. Three weeks later in Nanking, General Okamura formally signed the document.

It was a signal event in the Sino-Japanese War, a struggle in which the AVG Flying Tigers and their successors — the Flying Tigers of the Fourteenth Air Force — played a crucial role. The war was over; surrender taking its place. The combative General Chennault was firmly nudged into retirement. And my long-serving friends in the 397th were finally going home.

Utter desolation set the scene at Chihkiang Airfield for the arrival of representatives from the China Expeditionary Army (Imperial Japanese Army).

The Mitsubishi Ki-57, Allied code name "Topsy" (above), was a standard transport plane of the Japanese Army. While at Chihkiang, crews covered and secured the engines and wind screen during its brief stay.

Major General Takeo Imai, accompanied by two staff officers and one interpreter, arrived at Chihkiang Airfield on August 21, 1945, to receive the terms for surrender of all Japanese forces in China.

- 11 - *What Would Follow?*

The devastating war that began in 1931 in Manchuria, spreading to larger areas of China in 1937, was finally over. The Japanese would soon depart. But it became clear that the conflict between the Nationalist government of Chiang K'ai-shek and the Communists under Mao Tse-Tung would gain speed, further crushing Chinese society until only one side or the other survived. Both had long been waiting to get at each other. They had killed each other for far too long to make peace now.

For the next few weeks, there was increased activity at Chihkiang. Planes of the Air Transport Command, and others belonging to the Chinese air force, began a speeded-up program transferring tens of thousands of Chinese soldiers to northern cities; many of these flights funneled through Chihkiang. The accelerated schedule led to crashes and countless deaths.

One night my tent mates and I were roused from sleep by the approach of screaming, misfiring engines, signaling a plane in distress. A Chinese transport moving soldiers north was careening in the general direction of our tent, located uncomfortably close to the runway. As I bolted from bed, my instinct should have been to duck and run. Instead, I froze in place.

The doomed plane roared overhead; sounds of hell spewed from its engines. It crashed into the large hill to the rear of our tent; a spectacular explosion blew the plane apart and flames lit up the sky. There was little we could do. A fire truck was on its way. The following morning there were few human remains in the ruins larger than a charred, still smoking foot.

Chiang K'ai-shek, with support from the United Sates, attempted to forestall the occupation of China's northern cities by Communist armies; the latter had moved quickly from their power centers in that part of the country. Chiang's Nationalist forces, representing the recognized government of China, openly challenged the growing Communist threat, just as they had after the failure of previous alliances promoted by the American government. Attempts at cooperation between these former grudging allies, now turned deadly enemies, met with little success.

Each side wanted to rule without the other. Many of us on the scene had little doubt a general war was inevitable. Either the Nationalists or the Communists would survive as a controlling force. It was unlikely Chiang and his government could win. The people, it seemed to me, did not support the Generalissimo. Whenever, through translators, one spoke of Chiang to the Chinese, their reactions usually were negative. Many would spit on the ground at the mention of his name.

Their actions reflected their contempt for the Soong family, a political and financial powerhouse in China. Soong Mei-ling, one of three Soong sisters, had married Chiang K'ai-shek and helped his rise to power through her family connections and her undeniable charm, beauty, and intelligence.

Her sister, Soong Ching-ling, was the wife of Sun Yat-sen, first provisional president of the Republic of China (1912) and a man still highly respected. Mme Chiang's brother, T. V. Soong (Soong Tse-ven/Paul Soong), was governor of the Central Bank of China, and Finance Minister under Chiang. He wielded great financial power, but many of the common people, the only ones I personally knew, believed he was thoroughly corrupt and had corrupted Chiang.

The people seemed to say, by their anger and their spitting, that the Soongs and their cronies, including Chiang himself, were accumulating power and wealth without much regard for the interests and welfare of the Chinese people.

Chiang may not have deserved that reputation — he appeared to be a fierce patriot. But he seemed to have no organized system of political beliefs by which a nation like China, with its ancient culture, could begin its long journey into the modern world. He took the only road he knew: he became the warlord-in-chief, ruling through the allegiance of mostly corrupt, regional satraps, military men with their own armies, their own interests; men whose principal roles were collecting taxes (only some of which they turned over to Chiang's government) and maintaining regional authority through violence.

It was an old Chinese system similar to European practices during the Middle Ages. It was a China of poor, mostly illiterate, often disease-ridden peasants, bound to powerful landlords who controlled their lives and shackled them to the past.

I had a strong foreboding while stationed in Peishiyi and Chihkiang, and during our week-long convoy through villages, small towns and hamlets. I believed that the Communists would eventually rule China. The brooding negativism about Chiang's central government, when compared with reports of spreading Communist influence among the people, gave little cause for optimism. Whatever Washington bureaucrats may have thought, as they talked ... and talked ... and argued among themselves,

American opposition to the Communists had no effect whatsoever on the ordinary Chinese people. They were not even aware of it. In the meantime, the Communists moved among the masses, shared their lives, explained their programs, and handed guns to these new common allies.

The bitter adversaries, Mao Tse-Tung (above), seen on 4 December 1944, and (left) Generalissimo Chiang K'ai-Shek, visiting a military base in March 1945

- 12 - *Next, to Hankow*

A few weeks after the final surrender, I was one of twenty-two or twenty-three men from the 397th Squadron flown to the Japanese-held city of Hankow. We were told the Japanese garrison of 75,000 to 100,000 soldiers had accepted the final surrender and put down their arms. Hankow had been the command center of Japanese armed forces in the Yangtze River basin and the rest of south China. In all, close to a million men, perhaps more.

Our mission, as I remember it, was to establish American operational control of the air base, to assist planes in transit, and to organize a depot for incoming supplies. I was never aware of other G.I.s on the base; we saw no American soldiers other than aircrews shuttling in a growing mountain of supplies. While some of our contingent began servicing incoming American and some Chinese aircraft, and maintaining radio communications, I was among those warehousing the incoming supplies. Under our direction, hired Chinese laborers did the physical work. I kept the books.

As long as we stayed at the airfield, we saw very few Japanese soldiers. Yet just knowing that our small group from the 397th was submerged in a sea of former enemies, many of them merciless, was a sobering thought. One question arose: what would happen if the Japanese, perhaps under a renegade commander, ignored the surrender and decided to resume the war in China, fighting to the death. In retrospect, it was an unlikely scenario.

I never considered my time overseas to be overly hazardous to survival; after all, it was wartime and the important thing was to remain alive. I was lucky as hell. I was never shot at, although one nearby ammo dump exploded, raining debris, large and small, on some of us. I was never in an aircraft that crashed or was damaged. I usually ate three meals a day, not always good ones; had a cot on which to sleep most nights. Sickness came with the assignment, but that was not the same as combat. Some men in the 397th did die in aircraft and truck accidents; some, I was told, went down in a plane crash while flying over the Himalayas. A few men died of illnesses, one officer from a rat bite. Personally, my only medical problems thus far had been a single case of leg infection in India, and frequent fever, dysentery, and attacks of malaria repressed by Atabrine but making me want to curl up and die. Not bad for a long war in which, yes, I *had* been incredibly lucky.

When we arrived in Hankow, we were quickly faced with a flood of supplies that began filling up our warehouses, including some quality items none of us had seen in China. No one understood the purpose of these shipments but, as usual, everyone had an opinion: Hankow was to become a base for an enlarged U.S. Air Force in China, perhaps for a role in the coming civil war between Communists and Nationalists; or maybe we were preparing a major base for the Chinese air force. Maybe this. Maybe that. But as the flow of supplies continued unabated, it was certain that nobody knew what the hell we all were talking about.

Four of the guys decided to improve their standard of living by storing a few of the incoming items in a large tent they erected for themselves. Placed close to the main warehouse, the tent was furnished with a variety of items from this overflowing cornucopia, including four comfortable hospital beds, generator-powered reading lamps, one for each man; several cases of Scotch and rye whiskey labeled "medical alcohol" — short wave radios, real American coffee, canned rations like none ever seen, or eaten; a first rate portable electric stove, and other items since forgotten. Each man signed out his own Jeep.

Anything they could use was put on "detached service" in their ever more comfortable living quarters. Incoming American air crews, hearing about this comfortable island in a Japanese sea, began dropping by for a drink or two, followed by warm meals of surprisingly good food. This bountiful haven was fully shared with fellow Americans, whatever rank or status. As sometimes stated, supply sergeants seemed to make the army work more efficiently.

Now and then a few soldiers ventured out of our restricted base into a virtual no-mans land, driving a few miles into the center of Hankow for a good civilian meal, even though most restaurants were considered off limits. There were still more than 100,000 Japanese soldiers and civilians living among this overcrowded city's huge Chinese population.

Other foreigners lived there, too — hundreds of Europeans, perhaps thousands. Some had been trapped there by the war, others were longtime residents living there by choice. There was danger in this hostile city beyond the range of American protection, but it was vague and non-specific.

One evening, my buddies and I decided to have our first civilized dinner at a somewhat faded European-style hotel, one undoubtedly built in the previous century. The owner was a Frenchwoman a shade past her prime, somewhat like her hotel. To a young man of twenty-four, any woman over thirty-five seemed middle-aged. Her carefully coiffed frizzy hair framed a rather pretty face. Her Gallic personality was stirred by the presence of the Americans, and she soon joined us to celebrate the end of hostilities.

Hankow had been this woman's home for years — I remember wondering if she would ever leave. Bubbling with conversation, she recounted a number of stories about the Japanese occupation. A few hours in, our interest slackened; I am sure a couple of my friends were more interested in the woman than her stories. To close out the evening, our hostess produced dust-covered bottles of French liqueurs. I remember consuming more than my share of Cointreau.

We were the first 'victorious' Americans this lady had seen. Her disdain for the Chinese was clear: "They are dirty," she said; "stupid and treacherous," she said. She thought the Japanese were just fine. We later decided a protective Japanese officer, a close friend, was probably the reason for her attitude. Hadn't she heard about the slaughter at Nanking, or the other atrocities of the past eight years? But at the time, her forgiving attitude toward our former enemy was of little concern to us. We were out of the rice paddies, no longer dependent on water buffalo meat dragged through the dirt. Now we were dining in style, drinking French cordials with a spirited French woman who looked prettier after each drink. At the time, anything seemed possible.

Every day, by the tens of thousands, Japanese soldiers marched, or walked, in long formations that snaked along primitive roads near the airfield. Some of their officers carried Samurai swords, many of the enlisted men still carried rifles. They were completely docile, accepting defeat. The Emperor had ordered them to surrender, and they had done so. Without a whimper, they obeyed; women and children, too, presumably families of Japanese army officers and civilian administrators. They were polite and well mannered.

A growing number of American planes began using the Hankow airfield. They transported Chiang K'ai-shek's divisions north to oppose the spreading Communist takeover. It was clear from everything we heard that the Reds were well organized and were quickly asserting control over a population well disposed to their ideas. The little co-operation that previously existed between the two Chinese factions dissolved when they no longer had a common foe. The Communists had a tacit understanding with the Japanese that kept the fighting between them to a minimum, while Chiang's Nationalist armies shouldered the brunt of the conflict. The Communist revolution spread, opposing Chiang's weak and disorganized government. At its peril, the United States was getting much too involved.

As I recall, most of my companions were only marginally interested in the political conflict at hand. My own interest in world affairs and politics was renewed as news of the world became more available. In China, we were witnessing the evolution of a new world power — one, it seemed, destined to reclaim its former greatness. The later political arguments in the U.S. over "who lost China?" always seemed beside the point, foolish, and politically inspired. China was never ours to lose; that was a matter the

Chinese people would — and did — decide for themselves. But at the time, as many veterans of the 397th were already doing, my main interest centered on the craving to go home.

In the early days of December, I developed a high fever and felt miserable. I was flown to Shanghai for medical attention and, after shivering for several hours in an unheated tent, was admitted to an Army hospital.

At that point, my recent life simply dissolved from the screen ... farm fields and rice paddies; my comrades in the 397th Squadron; Hankow, with its airfield, airplanes and 75,000 sullen Japanese soldiers; my friends' comfortable, well-equipped tent with its supplies of "medical alcohol" — all of it went blank. Survival became my sole concern. My personal things were forwarded to me in a duffel bag by one of my tent mates ... Army clothes, some letters, a razor and toothbrush, and my prized photos of China.

The diagnosis was paratyphoid fever, or maybe typhoid itself; both were mentioned, interchangeably. I had seen too many Chinese die of these sicknesses to be unconcerned. For several nights and days, I shivered with chills and burned with fever, each following the other every fifteen or twenty minutes. I was told the walls of my intestinal tract had been thinned by the infection and could be punctured by solid foods. With a steady diet of thin soups and cold liquids, my weight fell to under 160 pounds.

But hospital care was good, the Army nurses attentive, and by the end of December I was feeling better, gaining weight and beginning once again to think about the future. I was told I would not be returning to my outfit in Hankow ... instead, I would be released into a pool of G.I.s awaiting shipment back to the States. But first, I had to get back on my feet. That would take time, more than the five weeks spent in the hospital. When discharged, my fighting weight was 162 pounds.

The cantankerous Lt. General Claire Lee Chennault (1)

In their battle against Japanese invaders in the second Sino-Japanese War, China recruited Claire Chennault to take charge of its fledgling air force. About this job Chennault wrote to his brother, William: "It may amount to very little except a good paying position, but it may amount to a great deal ... it is even possible that my 'feeble' efforts may influence history."
Chennault Aviation and Military Museum, Monroe, Louisiana

- 13 - *Waiting in Shanghai*

In mid-January 1946, I was assigned to an 'awaiting' unit in Shanghai. That was the good news. The less-than-good news: it wasn't until mid-March before several thousands of us, most meeting the requirements of a complicated priority point system, shipped out on the *USS General H. L. Scott*. Destination, Seattle.

Through the long weeks of impatient delay, I worked in some nondescript army office, in no way memorable for its staff or the work we presumably did. I recall nothing about it, nothing. On the other hand, I remember nearly everything about my off-duty hours in Shanghai, and those spent with new friends. Some of them were American soldiers; others were long-time civilian refugees from Nazi Germany and the Soviet Union. Some were White Russians who fled the Communist Revolution and settled safely in China in the years following the 1919 uprisings in St. Petersburg. Or so they said.

My closest companion in liberated Shanghai was Sidney, my warm-hearted friend from our days in Chihkiang, the kindly benefactor of our Belgian nuns and their young novices. Like so many of us, Sidney was awaiting shipment home. Somehow or other, he had found me in the military hospital and came to visit two or three times. Following my release shortly after New Year's Day '46, he and I were nearly inseparable for almost two months. Sidney took me to a Jewish synagogue for a religious service; I took him to a Chinese opera — a first for each of us.

Another acquaintance was Hans, a Jewish refugee from Nazi Germany. He had escaped the Gestapo, together with his wife and her elderly parents, only to be interned in a bleak ghetto set up by the Japanese to confine European Jews at the behest of their Axis partner, Germany.

When I met Hans, he was a civilian truck driver recently employed by the American army. How he and his family survived during the war remained a mystery. When invited to his small, one room apartment where he and his family lived, I found Hans relentless in seeking my help to gain entry to the United States. There was nothing I could do, and repeatedly told him so. I could only offer friendship and a few gifts to ease his family's plight.

Jews — thousands of them — living in the Shanghai ghetto during Japanese occupation suffered harsh privation and sometimes physical abuse. Most survived; others died from hunger and the prison-like conditions surrounding them. Japanese treatment of the Jews never matched the Nazi's fanatical hatred; rather, it seemed their impersonal abusiveness reflected a widespread absence of human feelings for anyone not of their race.

Seeing Hans and his family in their sparse surroundings was painful. His wife's parents huddled on a narrow cot beneath a blanket on cold winter days or evenings, shivering in their drab, unheated room. Until Hans received his first paycheck from the army, he and his family had very little to live on. Nevertheless, he offered me such hospitality as his circumstances permitted — an unpeeled orange, a glass of cheap potato vodka.

It appeared that his lovely wife was being proffered as a gift as well, an inducement for me to help the family reach America. She sometimes walked with me after a visit to their home, making painfully clear her wish to be friendly. It was all so sad. I like to think that Hans and his wife later found a way to reach America, at a cost that was not too great. Perhaps, in their circumstances, no price was too great.

With Japan's defeat, and the arrival in Shanghai of American military personnel, Jews were no longer restricted to the ghetto, though most of them continued to live there until their incomes generated savings. Some found a way to go elsewhere. Unable to find work with American occupation forces, many Jews just continued to survive in any way they could.

Sidney and I became friendly with a German doctor and his wife, a Jewish couple descended from generations of German professionals. They were living in the ghetto with the other interned Jews. This couple had found their way to Shanghai after fleeing Germany in the mid-Thirties, initially seeking protection in the International Settlement, a large section of the city that remained under European control. When the Second Sino-Japanese war erupted in 1937, the European soldiers protecting the International Settlement were forced to leave. Again, Jews found themselves in a ghetto and under the control of an Axis partner.

The doctor and his wife told us that at home in Europe, they had almost forgotten their Jewish heritage and religion, thinking of themselves only as Germans. They were horrified to be persecuted by the Nazis for their ancestral Jewish blood. Fleeing with their young son to Shanghai by steamship in 1935, they were rounded up by the invading Japanese two years later, together with thousands of other Jewish refugees. Their situation improved when the doctor's medical skills became known to other Jewish families, to the Japanese, and to some of the Chinese collaborators. The doctor attracted patients from all of these groups.

Our new friends believed that everyone had to survive, even if that meant cooperating with the Japanese by providing them medical attention. They lived somewhat more comfortably than most of the interred Jews, had better food, and a much better apartment; they even had an amah — a Chinese nanny — for their son. It was easy to disagree with the decisions some of these people made. I could not. I hadn't walked in their shoes.

The several White Russians that we also befriended had fled their mother country early in the 1920s, and now, more than a decade later, they too were virtual prisoners in Shanghai. Some of them came to China as children and were now adults. One of them from the synagogue was an attractive, highly intelligent young woman who, as a child, left Russia with her parents. Perhaps inertia rooted her to Shanghai — after all, she had spent most of her life there; it was her home. What other options did she have? The Japanese invasion and occupation sealed her fate.

After a rambling conversation with Sidney and me, fueled by a few drinks, this raven-haired Jewish beauty revealed that she had survived for years by keeping company with Japanese officers. She felt stained by the experience, or so she claimed. (Then again, she may have considered us the next potential consorts.)

After having been warehoused in the hospital for more than a month, I was intoxicated by exposure to the full array of Chinese people and culture. Shanghai seemed again destined to become the busy, throbbing heart of Asia. The city was a manufacturing and financial center still driven by energy unleashed during its former European occupation, still fueled by the enterprise and energy of the Chinese people.

Secure in knowing I would soon be returning to my home and family, I embraced everything Chinese — enjoying the good, observing the bad; there was plenty of both. I wanted to experience all of it. Smiling Chinese men and women, released from the chains of Japanese occupation, were not fully aware of, or chose to ignore, the deadly Red cloud approaching from the north.

A few thousand CBI veterans were in Shanghai, going through the motions of performing temporary duties while preparing to return home. Sailors from American warships fanned out in the bustling city. Dance halls were filled at night with very tiny, very shy Chinese women. Many of these young women were available as companions for a few dollars, some of them disappearing to their rooms or down dark alleys with young sailors determined to prove their manhood by these brief conquests.

The lilting music of China was heard everywhere; I had listened to these sing-song melodies on radio stations broadcasting from Chungking and Kunming. Everywhere, everything was for sale. Inflation and occupation had destroyed the value of Chinese currency. Everyone wanted American dollars.

It was all part of an electrifying marketplace. But beneath the city's brightly lit facade, the planning and plotting of Nationalists and Communists intensified. They were implacable enemies, each with a fervor that matched religious fanaticism. In spite of American diplomacy, the two sides never seriously joined in a search for peace; too many on each side had been killed.

Chiang K'ai-shek's soldiers were now in charge of Shanghai and most of southern and central China. But Mao's well-organized cadres had taken control of the north and were relentlessly and successfully organizing everywhere. They were moving swiftly to supplant the Nationalist government in areas they did not already control. Regrettably, my friends and I spent too little time thinking about China's future or Communism's uncompromising advance, unaware that the tectonic plates of history were shifting literally beneath our feet.

One final memory of China remains with me, crystal clear. Some weeks before leaving Shanghai, I stood in a massive crowd of Chinese people, engulfed by more than 100,000 cheering men, women, and children. They were gathered on the grounds of the city's huge racetrack to celebrate Generalissimo Chiang K'ai-shek's final victory over the Japanese invaders.

Chiang and his wife were there, standing behind a microphone on the speaker's platform, joined by various other dignitaries. General Wedemeyer was standing next to Chiang. I believe General George Marshal was there as well.

With a friend, I snaked forward in the grandstand to reach a spot close to Chiang. Looking out over the multitude, it was a breathtaking view. It captured the latent power of China's enormous population, organized efficiently in different groups of thousands, each massed phalanx holding a different banner.

They marched, on command, to assigned positions. Again on command and in unison, these thousands of celebrants began singing an anthem and waving their banners. I remember thinking that if the people of China coalesced into a single, unified country — without the constraints imposed by individualism and free expression — no power on earth could withstand them. In 1946, the Chinese population was said to be about 550 million. In 2006, the number was more than double that. During those fifty years, the intelligence and talent of the Chinese people had been organized into a unified population destined to play a major role in contemporary world history, as evidenced today.

A Jewish girl and her Chinese friends in the Shanghai Ghetto, China (1)

Shanghai's Ohel Moishe Synagogue was designed and built in the 1920's to accommodate a growing congregation originally established by Russian immigrants in 1907. During the Japanese occupation of Shanghai, a number of Jewish refugees were able to live there, including W. Michael Blumenthal, who, at age ten, escaped Nazi Germany with his family in 1939. Blumenthal eventually served as U.S. Secretary of the Treasury (1977-79) in the Carter administration. The synagogue was confiscated in 1949 after the communist takeover, and converted to government use. In 2007, the structure was restored to its original architectural design and opened as the Shanghai Jewish Refugees Museum. Photo: Harvey Barrison (2)

Designed and built in the 1920s by the firm Palmer and Turner (currently P&T Architects & Engineers Ltd / Hong Kong), Beth Aharon Synagogue was established in the Shanghai International Settlement by businessman Silas Aaron Hardoon as a tribute to his father. During World War II, the synagogue offered refuge to the Mir yeshiva after its escape from the Nazi occupation of Poland. In later years the structure was converted to industrial use and was eventually demolished in 1985 to make way for a high-rise office building. (3)

Japanese Special Naval Landing Force troops are seen marching into the Shanghai International Settlement, China, December 8, 1941 (4)

Allied victory drive along Nanking Road in Shanghai (5)

- 14 - *Heading Home*

It was time to go home. Several thousand American G.I.s boarded the *USS General H. L. Scott*, a troop transport much like the *General McRae* that delivered me to Calcutta more than fourteen months earlier. The war was over. I would be home in a few weeks. I was going to rejoin my family and — as with the rest of the returning G.I.s — pick up the strands of my life.

In Europe, the German juggernaut had been crushed — the surrender was unconditional. The charred remains of Adolph Hitler mirrored his burned out German Reich. I had witnessed Japan's withdrawal in southern and central China, and been present at Chihkiang for the final surrender of Japanese forces. Meanwhile, Douglas MacArthur and his divisions had been sweeping across the Pacific until they were poised for a final assault on the Japanese homeland, the citadel that would be defended to the last man, or so we believed. The climactic, shocking atomic bombing that obliterated most of Hiroshima and Nagasaki had consigned a conquest-seeking Imperial Japan to history. For now, all the wars were over.

The fourteen-day voyage home was a time for contemplation, a time to reflect on the meaning of the past three-and-a-half years ... their meaning to me — to all of us. It was a time to consider how I would use the years that were ahead of me. But I was young; my vision less than prophetic, or introspective. In spite of inconveniences and occasional sickness, I experienced no injuries in combat — no one had shot at me intending to kill. I had been very lucky, and I knew it.

March 20, 1946, our ship arrived at the port of Seattle. We were home. The troop train taking hundreds of us across the continent passed through the Northwest territories with stunning views of forests, mountains, rivers and waterfalls — then along miles of Canadian track winding through equally magnificent country. Tomorrow was all I could think about, and all the tomorrows to follow.

In the army discharge center at Fort Jay, New Jersey, a few days were consumed by interviews, paper work, medical exams — and, finally, a brief session with the paymaster. He gave me $181.29, including $100 mustering-out pay, fourteen days regular pay, and a $5 travel allowance, barely enough to get me to New York City. I was given final discharge papers, an invitation to join the reserves, a printed message of gratitude from President Harry S. Truman, and a ruptured duck pin to wear in my lapel. Still dressed in my uniform, with a newly tailored Eisenhower jacket, I boarded a train headed for New York City. I had been in the Army Air Force three-and-a-half years — to the day.

In that horrific war, thousands of my compatriots were far, far less fortunate than I was. They were the supreme heroes. Honor them all.

USS General H. L. Scott (AP-136) (1)

World War II Memorial
Washington, D.C.

Ending Note

It seemed strange that my isolation as a boy growing up in suburban Long Island, New York, ended in a remote, unknown place in the far reaches of China. Nothing, absolutely nothing, had prepared me for this powerful immersion into the real world. I venture to say that a great many of my fellow American men and women in uniform were unprepared, as well. We all grew up, fast.

My recollections of this period in my life were sparked by a recent perusal of the small collection of photographs that I brought home with me. A number of them appear in this book. These photographs picture not only military scenes, they also record the pervasive and insidious battle being waged at the time, day-by-day, by the Chinese people, merely to eat, to work; simply to remain alive.

The memory was further brought back by an eight-page letter written to my wife and parents a few days after the bombing of Hiroshima, and by descriptions found in Theodore White's excellent autobiography, *In Search of History*.

Bernard Naltby's book, *Tigers Over Asia* was a great read, too; as was *Baa Baa Black Sheep*, written after the war by Major Pappy Boyington, one of the original Flying Tigers and later a Marine Corps flying ace.

Yet despite the best of intentions in compiling this narrative, it is likely that I have made some mistakes in certain details, or in the events I have described and their proper sequence. If so, the miscues are not by design.

REY
June 2010

Profile of U.S. Servicemen — 1941-1945

- 38.8% (6,332,000) of U.S. servicemen and all servicewomen were volunteers
- 61.2% (11,535,000) were draftees
- Average duration of service: 33 months
- Overseas service: 73% served overseas. Average 16 months abroad.
- Combat survivability (out of 1,000):
    8.6 killed in action
    3 died from other causes
    17.7 received non-fatal combat wounds
- Non-combat jobs: 38.8% of enlisted personnel had rear echelon assignments
- Average base pay:
    Enlisted — $71.33 per month
    Officer — $203.50 per month

Source: National World War II Museum, New Orleans, Louisiana

Addendum

CHINA OFFENSIVE:

The U.S. Army Campaigns of World War II
Theresa L. Kraus, U.S. Army Center of Military History
CMH Publication 72-39

"On 22 August 1945, the China Theater suspended all training under American supervision, an action that marked the beginning of the end for the elaborate system of American liaison, air and logistical support, and advice. The armies of Chiang Kai-shek would soon be on their own."

"The American advisory effort in China not only aided the Allied military effort, but also reinforced traditional United States interests in China. From the beginning of the war, President Roosevelt wanted to bolster Chiang and the Nationalist government to serve as a counterpoint against a potentially resurgent Japan. The President saw postwar China as a major power and partner, protecting U.S. economic, diplomatic, and strategic interests in Asia. Although the United States subsequently provided massive amounts of economic and military aid to Chiang Kai-shek, that assistance failed to create an effective, pro-Western government or military force. Within four years of the war's end Mao Tse-tung and his Communist forces overran China, forcing Chiang and his Nationalist supporters to flee to the island of Formosa and providing the last act in a drama that had begun forty years earlier."

WAR TORN CHINA
1940s

Collection: Robert Yost

Chinese-American Institute of Cultural Relations
Location: possibly Chungking

telegram: Washington, Nov 4, 1942, 9 p.m.
The Secretary of State to the Ambassador in China (Gauss)

"Your reports on the Chinese-American Institute of Cultural Relations seem to indicate that the institute is firmly established and is engaged in activities well calculated to promote cultural relations between the United States and China. The Department will welcome your suggestions for the supply to the institute of equipment that may not be obtainable in China such as motion picture projectors, educational films, books, magazines, microfilms and projectors and phonographs and records. Shipment of such articles would of course depend upon the availability of transportation facilities. The Embassy is hereby authorized to transfer this contribution to the institute in amounts and at times suggested by the institute up to a total of $18,000."
HULL [Cordell Hull]   Source: https://history.state.gov

WAR TORN CHINA - 1940S

(above) Lt. General Albert C. Wedemeyer, Commanding General of U.S. forces in the China theater and Chief of Staff to Chiang K'ai-shek, outside Headquarters, U.S. Forces, China Theater. Location believed to be the main command center in Chungking.

Location unknown

Fourteenth Air Force base at Kweilin, China, *(right)* was approximately 360 miles southeast of Chungking. November 1944, the airfield was evacuated and subsequently captured by the Japanese. It was successfully re-taken in July 1945 by Chinese forces, just prior to Japan's surrender at Chihkiang.

WAR TORN CHINA - 1940S

Locations unknown

Artisans, builders and craftsmen from earlier days left their marks on that part of China the American G.I.s passed through. In the midst of ruin there was still beauty – in the graceful architecture, in faded silk robes, in the gentle politeness that prevailed. *(above)* Note the silk robe, airing in the wind.

Locations unknown

Even in the circumstances of a brutal, devastating war, the Chinese people remained rooted in a framework of centuries-old life, a life virtually unknown to the average American at the time.

Locations unknown

Locations unknown

WAR TORN CHINA - 1940S

Locations unknown

Kunming, China

Location unknown

Location and identity unknown

The gentle, industrious and orderly Chinese people had the ability to smile easily. They were not formed by opposing Nationalist or Communist philosophies, but were descended from an earlier civilization — the centuries of old Cathay.

Locations unknown

Historically, the family rather than the individual or the state formed the primary unit in Chinese society. The highest virtues and greatest social satisfactions were attached to the structure and hierarchy of family life, and to a deep reverence for family forebears.

Location unknown

WAR TORN CHINA - 1940S

Locations unknown

WAR TORN CHINA - 1940S

Location unknown

Locations unknown

Location unknown

WAR TORN CHINA - 1940S

Locations unknown

Locations unknown

Location and identities unknown

Location and identities unknown

Just as it was for millennia.

Location unknown

Images

Chapter 2
1. Army Air Force truck convoy passing through Miami Beach. Postcard, 1943
U.S. Army Air Forces, AAF
*https://commons.wikimedia.org/wiki/File:Army_Air_Forces_-
_Postcard_Miami_Beach_Training_Center_-_AAF_Truck_Convoy*

Chapter 3
1. General Anthony Clement McAuliffe
*https://www.archives.gov/exhibit_hall/a_people_at_war/war_in_europe/images_war_in_europe/
general_mcauliffe.jp*

Chapter 4
1. USS General G. O. Squier (AP-130), off the coast of California. Date unknown.
https://commons.wikimedia.org/wiki/File:USS_General_G.O._Squier_(AP-130).jpg

Chapter 5
1. Calcutta, India, 1945
*https://commons.wikimedia.org/wiki/
File:Corner_of_Harrison_Street_(Burra_Bazar)_and_Strand_Road,_Calcutta_in_1945.jpg*

Chapter 6
1. U.S. Army trucks on the Ledo Road, India
*Creator: Office for Emergency Management. Office of War Information. Overseas Operations
Branch. New York Office. News and Features Bureau. (12/17/1942 - 09/15/1945)
U.S. National Archives and Records Administration, NAID 535540
https://commons.wikimedia.org/wiki/File:
%22U.S.built_Army_trucks_wind_along_the_side_of_the_mountain_over_the_Ledo_supply_road_
now_open_from_India_into_Burma..%22_-_NARA_-_535540.jpg*

2. Chabua airfield, India, 1944
*United States Army Air Force via National Archives
https://commons.wikimedia.org/wiki/File:Chabuaaf-1944.jpg*

Chapter 11
1. Mao Tse-Tung, 6 December 1944
*Franklin D. Roosevelt Library (NLFDR), 4079 Albany Post Road, Hyde Park, NY, 12538-1999
U.S. National Archives and Records Administration, NAID 196235
https://commons.wikimedia.org/wiki/File:Mao_Tse-Tung,_leader_of_China
%27s_Communists,_addresses_some_of_his_followers._-_NARA_-_196235.tif*

2. Chiang Kai-skek, March 1945
https://commons.wikimedia.org/wiki/File:Chiang_Kai-shek_enhanced.jpg

Chapter 12
1. Lieutenant General Claire Chennault
https://commons.wikimedia.org/wiki/File:ClaireChennault.jpeg

Chapter 13
1. Girls of the Shanghai ghetto
Shanghai Jewish Refugees Museum collection
https://commons.wikimedia.org/wiki/File:Girls_of_the_Shanghai_Ghetto.png

2. Ohel Moishe Synagogue, Shanghai. Photographer: Harvey Barrison
Creative Commons Attribution-Share Alike 2.0 Generic
https://commons.wikimedia.org/wiki/File:Ohel_Moishe_Synagogue_Shanghai.jpg

3. Beth Aharon Synagogue, Shanghai, 1930s
https://commons.wikimedia.org/wiki/File:Beth_Aharon_Synagogue.jpg

4. Japanese Special Naval Landing Force troops marching into Shanghai International Settlement, China, 8 December 1941
Lava Development LLC, World War II Database, C. Peter Chen
https://ww2db.com/image.php?image_id=23917

5. Allied victory drive along Nanking Road, Shanghai
U.S. Army Military History Institute
https://history.army.mil/brochures/chinoff/chinoff.htm

Chapter 14
1. USS General H. L. Scott (AP-136)
U.S. Coast Guard Historian's Office
https://commons.wikimedia.org/wiki/File:USS_General_H_L_Scott_(AP-136).jpg